Changing the Curriculum

Edited by John F. Kerr

UNIVERSITY OF LONDON PRESS LTD

ISBN 0 340 09437 0 Unibook

University of London Press Ltd
St Paul's House, Warwick Lane, London EC4P 4AH

Printed and bound in Great Britain by
Hazell Watson and Viney Ltd, Aylesbury, Bucks

Contents

Introduction

CURRICULUM renewal has been a continuous and gradual process since schooling began. The rate of change over the past five years has increased at an unprecedented speed and fundamental developments in many areas of the curriculum are under way or imminent. Beginning with mathematics and science projects at primary and secondary school levels, reform is spreading to the humanities, social sciences and crafts. The movement has been embraced by the principal agencies which normally promote and control educational change in this country. The Schools Council has been the most influential and active national agent since 1964, working increasingly through the officers of the local education authorities. Associated loosely with this network are various grant-giving bodies, notably the Nuffield Foundation, as well as many groups formed by professional associations of teachers, universities and colleges of education.

There is no doubt then that we are due for a great wave of curriculum renewal in the next decade or so. Are we in sufficient control of this process? Can deliberate and conscious decisions be made about the precise direction in which we should move? It is characteristic of any reform movement in education that the enthusiasm of persuasive innovators unintentionally sets off the 'band-wagon' effect. To some extent, this is happening. It is not necessarily to be deprecated, but it is clear that some schools and individuals acquire the reputation of being progressive and successful simply because of their association with prestigious projects or institutions, just as some innovators collect unjustified criticism from reactionary quarters.

This kind of emotionally-charged wrangling hampers real progress and arises because we have no rational, coherent theory, or even a set of concepts, on which modifications to the curriculum can be based. Curriculum making has developed rather as a craft develops from long practical experience. Out-

moded techniques and materials tend to be retained. New ideas
are incorporated into the process without regard to the total
operation or to its future use. There is no planned strategy for
making curricular decisions or evaluating changes introduced.
The traditional subjects of the curriculum are like eggs in a
crate, each fitting snugly into a pre-designed space, isolated
from the rest. There is need to analyse the process of curriculum
planning and to identify the elements that should be the
determinants of curriculum design. The purpose of this volume
is to contribute to this analysis and discussion.

When Beauchamp[1] examined the status of curriculum
theory in America in 1961, he found there was 'no logical and
consciously identified set of constructs behind the language
being used' by curriculum workers. From the limited literature
available in this country at the present time, a similar conclusion might be drawn about the status of curriculum theory
in Britain. Indeed, although the urgent need for curriculum
theorists to define and use precise terms and to work out a
theoretical framework has been emphasized in America for at
least two decades, only limited progress has been made
towards the definition of a generally-accepted system. Much
of the dialogue has been about the relative importance of the
basic factors on which the planning and design of the curriculum
are based. There has been a tendency among curriculum workers
to seek support for a variety of curriculum theories from the
foundation disciplines of education – philosophy, sociology,
psychology and history. Thus, the view that the primary
school curriculum should be essentially child-centred and provide exploratory experiences to promote learning relies heavily
on certain psychological theories related to individual differences and learning; but, with equal conviction, the placing of
the disciplines of knowledge and cognitive processes at the
heart of the curriculum can be justified by the philosophical
analysts in education. The danger of borrowing selected
findings from philosophy or psychology or sociology for
prescriptive purposes in curriculum development is referred to
in the first paper. This tendency to select material for use as

factual evidence to support one's preconceived view does not do justice either to these disciplines or to education. It does not take account of the tentative, immature state of psychology and the social sciences. A design for a particular curriculum is not likely to result from the application of one theory or set of ideas. Curriculum workers need some conceptual structures for the identification of the problems on which decisions have to be made. Not until these questions have been precisely stated can appropriate guidance be expected from the educational disciplines.

The connection between making curriculum decisions, or curriculum planning, and the topics included under headings such as the philosophy of education, the sociology of education, the psychology of education and history of education, is of particular relevance to teacher training. In spite of years of effort on the part of teacher-trainers and others, the study of education for many teachers remains separate from the actual job of teaching children in a classroom – a dichotomy between theory and practice which stubbornly refuses to be resolved.

Thus, there are two main reasons for a reconsideration of the contribution which each of the educational disciplines can make to the theory and practice of curriculum development:

1. It can help curriculum workers to specify curriculum objectives and plan learning experiences by selecting from and making better use of the specialist knowledge of philosophers, psychologists, sociologists and others.

2. It can encourage the notion that the curriculum is the natural core for initial and in-service training courses for teachers so that it becomes the reason for the inclusion of selected topics from the separate disciplines and the integrating force for all the elements of the course.

It was mainly for the first of these reasons that a short series of public lectures was arranged during the spring term 1967 at the School of Education, University of Leicester. The idea of drawing attention to the contribution which the various disciplines might make to curriculum planning and development arose from the writer's inaugural lecture at Leicester University in January 1967. The lecture is reprinted[2] in this volume. It is followed by four papers which were written by well-known professors of education. Each of them deals with the relationship of a different discipline to curriculum study. No attempt was made to brief each contributor, except in general terms, so that differences in the interpretation of some of the concepts used are discernible. All the writers, however, are agreed on the principle that it is towards the clarification and attainment of curriculum objectives that each discipline should aim to contribute. Any list of objectives should be consistent with accepted psychological and sociological principles and stated in precise terms to enable exact communication to take place.

The papers are presented to provoke discussion rather than to give complete, definitive statements. It is hoped they will further critical analysis of the complex process of curriculum change. Thus, Professor Hirst picks out four areas for philosophical analysis – the nature of educational objectives, the interrelatedness of the objectives, the nature of curriculum activities, and the structure of the curriculum plan. Professor Musgrove looks at the curriculum as a social system and concludes that curricula should be appropriate to a far more flexible social and educational order. Professor Taylor extends some of the issues raised in his inaugural lecture[3] and, by reference to a considerable literature, deals with the populations, processes and products associated with the curriculum. He distinguishes sharply between the goals of psychological study and curriculum theory, and reiterates the warning to curriculum workers that the psychological theories and constructs which they use are 'on loan' from psychology and should not be abused to give a 'gloss of scientific respectability' to curriculum proposals. After suggesting that the contribution which history might make to the changing curriculum seems remote, Professor Charlton demonstrates through an examination of models, generality, objectivity and tradition in history that one's sensitivity can be raised to the forces at work in our society which shape schools and curricula. Curriculum theory becomes useless if we imagine that changes are 'uniform and regular, and happen at a predictable rate'. Through the inclusion of the 'time' factor into curriculum design, change would be built into the process.

The second suggestion referred to above, which is brought to light by these discussions, is that the curriculum could become the natural focus for courses in teacher education. The continual interaction between change and conservation in education is a familar phenomenon, but one which does not nowadays receive much attention. It may be that the process of conservation continues, as Nunn described it,[4] to be 'the driving wheel whose energy guarantees the stability of all human societies'; but, in a rapidly changing educational scene, it is liable to be a brake to which many established and familiar ideas cling simply because they are familiar. This is certainly true for much of the material in education courses at colleges and universities. There is a strong case for a reassessment of the content of courses in education in terms of the theoretical foundations for curriculum construction, so that the curriculum would move from the periphery to the nucleus to control and integrate the rest of the training programme.

Such a change might make us more aware of the limitations of the curriculum reform movement. Although some effective courses and materials are certainly being produced, the movement is not realizing its full potentiality. Attention tends to be focused on single subjects so that the curriculum programme looks much the same. It may be that some new subjects or combinations of related disciplines should replace part of the conventional material, so that the structure of the total field of knowledge and the range of experiences provided would be more comprehensive and relevant. Almost without exception, curriculum workers do not set out their objectives in realistic and clearly defined terms, and there is a lack of direction in planning. As a result, evaluative techniques tend to be poor. A more perceptive examination of the disciplines on which the study of education has come to rely is clearly indicated by these papers. Such an examination promises much for the future of curriculum development.

References

1   G. A. Beauchamp, *Curriculum Theory*, Kegg Press, Wilmette, Illinois, 1961, p. 111.
2   J. F. Kerr, *The Problem of Curriculum Reform*, Leicester University Press (pamphlet), 1967.
3   P. H. Taylor, 'Purpose and Structure in the Curriculum', *Educational Review*, vol. 19, No. 3, and vol. 20, No. 1.
4   Percy Nunn, *Education: Its Data and First Principles*, Edward Arnold, 1945 (3rd edition), p. 34.

The Problem of Curriculum Reform*

PAPER I

John F. Kerr

IT is not only in education that new ideas and new procedures move in an apparently random manner from one emphasis to another without any obvious signs that the progression has been planned or even anticipated. The turning-points in science, in history, in social development are so often the results of social crises or hunches or the chance emergence of an outstanding mind or personality. It is much the same in education. Why should real progress in education not be subject to more efficient planning and development? Perhaps we have not been sufficiently concerned with the basic determinants of effective learning. I am not even sure that we know what they are.

When public education was first provided in this country, the teachers were not well enough trained to decide what and how they should teach. The educational process was controlled centrally by the allocation to year-groups, which we called 'standards', of precise instructional units designed to give training in basic skills. School boards, inspectors, and even 'payment by results' for a short time, ensured conformity. The teachers worked hard to achieve some degree of professional autonomy and by the 1950s it was generally accepted they were free to decide what and how they should teach. Although by now local education authorities had statutory responsibility for secular instruction, they had willingly delegated this responsibility to individual teachers and schools. The general liberalizing effect on the education provided was perhaps most

* An inaugural lecture delivered in the University of Leicester on 12 January 1967.

evident in the increase of understanding and attention given to individual children – that is, towards a child-centred curriculum. In the meantime, the central government, having set aside much of its responsibility for what went on in the classroom, continued to exercise its authority through control of building programmes and school organization, including examinations. The curriculum received scant attention until about five years ago when, largely through the initiative of groups of teachers brought together as members of professional associations,[1] a curriculum renewal movement began. It is of interest to ask ourselves why the knowledge taught in schools had grown so outmoded and inflexible; why the national demand for change was delayed for so long. Had we misused our freedom to decide what should be taught? Had we been too much concerned with the child-centred philosophy? Certainly the rapid social changes resulting from advances in technology and automation and the alarming growth of knowledge are forces which should have influenced the schools – and indeed the universities – long before the present decade.

Through the support of grant-giving bodies, particularly the Nuffield Foundation, projects for curriculum reform started, for obvious social reasons, in mathematics and the sciences. Since the beginning of the Nuffield Science Teaching Project in December 1961 over £1 million has been spent. The Nuffield model for curriculum construction is becoming a standard pattern. Teams of school teachers, college lecturers and university consultants backed by advisory committees draft new programmes which are tried out in selected schools. As a result of feedback from the pupils and teachers, the courses are modified and put to more extensive trial before publication. A wide range of course material is produced, including guides for teachers, texts for pupils, reference books, laboratory notes and background readers; newly designed apparatus and equipment; films, charts and models; and test instruments designed to measure specific outcomes of the course. When the Department of Education and Science established the Schools Council for the Curriculum and Examinations in October 1964, it was official acknowledgment of the need to plan the curriculum and examinations with a view to the achievement of carefully defined ends. National projects in many areas of the school curriculum are now in hand, including a 'resources for learning' project, sponsored by the Nuffield Foundation, in which a study will be carried out of the ways of organizing work in schools so as to make the best use of teachers' skills, and of new developments in method and equipment. Further evidence of growing attention to a formerly neglected area of education has been the recent appointment by several universities to chairs of education of people whose main interest lies within the field of curriculum research and development.

At the practical and organizational levels, the new curricula promise to revolutionize English education. Better decisions should be made by teams about the selection and organization of the content of courses, and about the relative merits of different teaching methods. But these decisions, or most of them, result from persuasive discourse in which each member of the team draws on his experience and personal judgment to arrive at a consensus of opinion. Theory has not played an important part in bringing about curriculum change simply because a coherent theoretical framework capable of guiding curriculum design is lacking. To build order into the process, a greater infusion of theory, research and evaluation is essential.[2] The pattern and interrelationships among the various disciplines might be clarified by a theory of the curriculum. The field trials of the new programmes might be designed to conform most closely to the requirements of rigorous operational research. Evaluation might be used not just for the terminal assessment of pupil changes but also to produce independent evidence about the effectiveness of each stage of the course as it is developed. At present curriculum workers lack adequate frames of reference for the assessment of progress and for the correlation of research efforts. They need these theoretical tools but, because of the impetus with which the movement for curriculum renewal is forging ahead, they are unable to wait for the curriculum theorist to work out effective models on which the new curricula might be based. This is the subject of my paper – the problem of curriculum reform. How far is it possible to develop a curriculum theory? What are the most appropriate models to start with? How can we arrive at a consensus of view about educational objectives? How should we take account of individual differences in children? What are the contributions of philosophy, psychology, sociology and history to curriculum development? These are some of the matters which are being referred to collectively as 'curriculum studies' – a new field for educators in this country in spite of thirty years' pioneer work by the Americans.

Before an attempt can be made to examine the problem of curriculum improvement more closely, it is necessary to make clear the sense in which the term 'curriculum' is being used. The range of meanings given to the concept of curriculum has been one of the sources of confusion in curriculum study. Many writers use the term loosely as being synonymous with 'syllabus', 'courses of study', 'subjects' or even 'timetable'. In many Colleges of Education the word, by tradition, is associated with narrowly conceived short courses which deal mainly with the methods of teaching a particular subject. The definition of curriculum used by Elizabeth Maccia, whose work at Ohio State University will be referred to later, is 'presented instructional content', instruction being conceived very specifically as a function of the relation between teacher behaviour and pupil behaviour.[3] Beauchamp's working definition is 'a design of a social group for the educational experiences of their children in school',[4] an example of many interpretations based on the notion of 'experience' offered by Dewey. The more comprehensive meaning used in this lecture is *all the learning which is planned and guided by the school, whether it is carried on in groups or individually, inside or outside the school.*[5]

Consideration of this broad inclusive definition suggests that the curriculum may be divided into four interrelated components – curriculum objectives, knowledge, learning experiences and curriculum evaluation. The interrelatedness of

the four components may be represented by a regular tetra-hedron with a component at each vertex (Fig. 1). The value of this simple model of the curriculum is that it suggests four basic questions for use in the construction of a new curriculum.

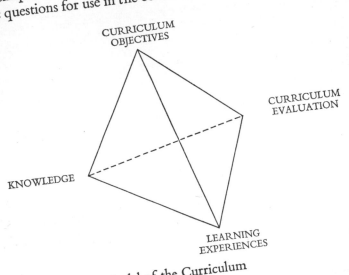

Fig. 1   A simple Model of the Curriculum

What is its purpose? What subject matter is to be used? What learning experiences and school organization are to be pro-vided? How are the results to be assessed? The model itse[l] gives no guidance about choice of objectives, content, methods of teaching. It does suggest facets of the curricul[um] which might be appropriate sources for the formulation [of] theory of the curriculum.

During recent years, the importance of theory as the [ ] for curriculum building has been stressed by many Am[erican] writers. It is apparent from the literature that there is co[ ] as to what theory is in this connection and how it can be [ ] to curriculum. The term 'theory' should not be use[d] scientific sense. We might legitimately use the ter[m] empirical sense, which includes speculation, especiall[y] relates to a number of hypotheses or a general background.

Two broad approaches to the building of curriculum theory, both in their infant stages, can be distinguished. The first is mainly deductive in that it involves taking theoretical formulations from other disciplines, substituting concepts, deducing hypotheses and laws, and testing the results against observable data. The work of Elizabeth Maccia and others since 1962 at the Ohio Educational Theory Centre is an example of the deductive approach. Maccia[6] states the meaning of theory in logical terms and identifies four kinds of theory: form theory, event (or reality) theory, valuational theory and, what she calls, praxiological theory or theory about practices. Each kind of theory is in turn used as a theory model from which a sub-theory of the curriculum is derived. So, formal curriculum theory gives meaning to the form of the main themes of a particular discipline, to its structure; curriculum reality (event) theory sets forth a group of propositions about content of instruction, how the component parts are interrelated and how they change; valuational curriculum theory is speculation as to curriculum objectives; and praxiological curriculum theory is speculation as to the appropriate means by which curriculum objectives can be achieved. From these four curriculum sub-theories, a curriculum theory model (Fig. 2) is constructed.[7]

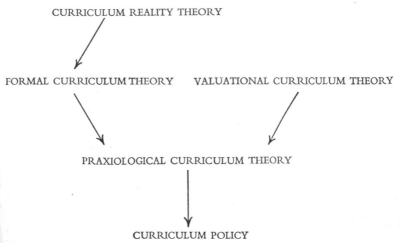

CURRICULUM REALITY THEORY

FORMAL CURRICULUM THEORY   VALUATIONAL CURRICULUM THEORY

PRAXIOLOGICAL CURRICULUM THEORY

CURRICULUM POLICY

Fig. 2   Maccia's Curriculum Theory Model

This particular theoretical framework has been criticized on the grounds that the methods of logic are not applicable to those human activities which are value-directed; and also that it does not provide for the evaluation of the curriculum. Educational theories do not as a rule have the logical bases which Maccia seems to be looking for.

In the second approach to the building of curriculum theory, referred to as the inductive approach, a synthetic method is adopted to build up a synoptic view of the curriculum from observable data. Assumptions and postulates are made which are basic to curriculum development, leading to prescriptions for curriculum design and evaluation. The stages or elements of this design guide curriculum choices. A criticism of this inductive approach is that one cannot approach data without theory – without some conceptual background to make selection from observed data possible: what Medawar referred to as the 'myth of the inductive method'.[8] Another drawback to this approach is that it results in a curriculum model which resembles a completed jig-saw puzzle. This is an unsatisfactory concept of curriculum. It ought to be a dynamic and con-tinuously-evolving system.

Professor Miel of Columbia University used a dynamic model based on a spiral to represent the path of change in educational thought.[9] The spiral was designed to enlarge as it ascended and represented a time line on which the major trends of thought were placed. It pictured not only the progression of events but also their interconnectedness and the way in which particular trends recur in a more sophisticated form than they had on the lower levels of the spiral. This model might be adapted to induce a synoptic view of the curriculum by representing curriculum objectives, knowledge and learning experiences as three intertwined threads of the spiral. Development of these curriculum components is clearly not as uniform a process as suggested by the spiral analogy. It would not be appropriate at this point to develop the spiral model, though it might be a fruitful exercise some time to do so.

Although we are not yet, manifestly, in a position to present
an acceptable model *of* [10] a curriculum theory, it is feasible, I
think, to build up a model *for* the curriculum, that is, for 'all
the learning which is planned and guided by the school . . .'
Such a model could encourage the development of sub-theories
of the identified components of the curriculum and perhaps
show the way towards a unified theory. It is proposed to
attempt a synthesis of such a model in brief outline, dealing
with objectives, evaluation, knowledge and learning experiences in turn, and then to consider the implications of the
model, especially for curriculum renewal and the in-service
education of teachers. As far as possible, I shall develop the
model in specific operational terms rather than in conceptual
terms. The infinitely complex nature of the curriculum, with
its many interdependent facets, makes it impossible to produce
more than a blurred image of the reality, especially in the time
available (see Fig. 3).

Commonly, curriculum discussion in schools, colleges and
universities is about the content of syllabuses and methods of
teaching. The really important questions are about objectives
and this component of the curriculum is the logical starting

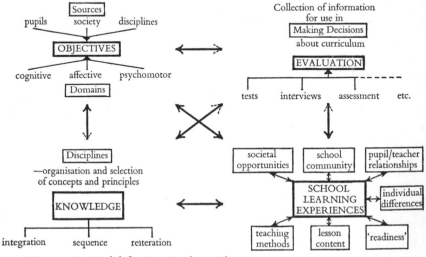

Fig. 3   A Model for Curriculum Theory

point, although one could break into the cycle of interrelated parts at any point. For the purposes of curriculum design and planning, it is imperative that the objectives should be identified first, as we cannot, or should not, decide 'what' or 'how' to teach in any situation until we know 'why' we are doing it. The task of identifying objectives calls for precise thinking and is a difficult exercise. Thus, few would disagree with Richard Peters's view that 'education is initiation into worthwhile activities', but before such a generalized statement can be useful to the curriculum builder, we must decide what is 'worthwhile'. In his inaugural lecture in 1965, Professor Bantock[11] was more specific, and therefore helpful to the curriculum builder, when he said that the ultimate purpose of education is 'clarification of the world of nature, of the world of man, and of the internal world of sensation and reflection, of emotion and cognition'. For curriculum purposes, the term 'objectives' is being used in a sense which was first formulated by R. W. Tyler[12] in 1933; that is, as changes in pupil behaviour which it is intended to bring about by learning. Teachers have in mind certain cognitive skills, attitudes and interests which they encourage pupils to acquire by the provision of appropriate learning experiences. It is in this sense that we speak of curriculum objectives as the intended outcomes of learning. So, a curriculum objective is a more conditional specification than an educational aim. An aim is no more than a target, but there are operational criteria associated with an objective; that is, the pupil must have been or will be involved in a particular kind of behaviour if the objective has been achieved.

In the construction or reconstruction of any part of the curriculum, decisions are made at each stage of the development which are based on the extent to which it is thought the stated objectives, if they have been made explicit, are being achieved. These decisions are too often reached on the basis of personal impression or, at best, consensus of opinion. We need to collect and use more valid and reliable data for this purpose. This is the object of curriculum evaluation. Since without evaluation we cannot be sure that the proposed objectives are attainable, the evaluation component of the curriculum is inseparable from the objectives component.

The formulation of specific and detailed curriculum objectives which are appropriate to a stated age range and social environment, as I have already suggested, is a difficult exercise. The objectives may be derived from three main sources of data. Information about the level of development of the pupils, their needs and interests, must be taken into account. The social conditions and problems which the children are likely to encounter provide a second source of data. And thirdly, there is the nature of the subject matter and types of learning which can arise from study of the subject matter. All the agencies concerned with the curriculum development should be involved in the production of a working list of objectives derived from these three sources. The final selection and sequence of the objectives should be feasible in terms of currently accepted educational principles.

The work of Bloom and his co-workers on educational objectives is highly significant for curriculum study. The two handbooks[13] which they have compiled provide a taxonomy of objectives in terms of student behaviour which is divided into two major classes or domains: the cognitive and the affective. A third group is recognized but has not been developed. This is the psychomotor domain which covers the manipulative or motor skill area. Behaviours are arranged from the simplest to the most complex, primarily from the curriculum viewpoint. Thus, in the cognitive domain ways of remembering, reasoning, problem solving and forming concepts are used to construct a detailed taxonomy based on levels of understanding. The classification ranges from the simplest knowledge of specific facts to the understanding and judgment of abstract theories and evidence (see Fig. 4). These are the distinctions which we claim to make when we teach. They are also the goals which should be tested. The affective domain is concerned with objectives related to interests, attitudes, values, appreciations and emotional sets. They range from simple attention to selected phenomena to complex relationships. In this case, the taxonomy is based on a complex and multidimensional concept known as 'internalization' through which, as defined by Bloom, 'there is at first an incomplete and tentative adoption of only the overt manifestations of the desired behaviour and later a more complete adoption'.[14] 'Willingness to attend' is at the lowest level of the affective scale. This scale extends to those objectives which characterize the individual almost completely – his philosophy of life and view of the universe (see Fig. 5). The separation of educational objectives into cognitive and affective classes is an artificial division, but it is sometimes convenient for the purposes of curriculum construction and evaluation to consider them separately.

1.0 KNOWLEDGE
    1.1 Knowledge of specifics
    1.2 Knowledge of ways and means of dealing with specifics
    1.3 Knowledge of universals and abstractions in a field
2.0 COMPREHENSION
    2.1 Translation
    2.2 Interpretation
    2.3 Extrapolation
3.0 APPLICATION
4.0 ANALYSIS
    4.1 Analysis of elements
    4.2 Analysis of relationships
    4.3 Analysis of organizational principles
5.0 SYNTHESIS
    5.1 Production of unique communication
    5.2 Production of a plan or a proposed set of operations
    5.3 Derivation of a set of abstract relations
6.0 EVALUATION
    6.1 Judgment in terms of internal evidence
    6.2 Judgment in terms of external criteria

Fig. 4 Summary of the Cognitive Domain

1.0   RECEIVING (attending)
    1.1   Awareness
    1.2   Willingness to receive
    1.3   Controlled or selected attention
2.0   RESPONDING
    2.1   Acquiescence in responding
    2.2   Willingness to respond
    2.3   Satisfaction in response
3.0   VALUING
    3.1   Acceptance of a value
    3.2   Preference for a value
    3.3   Commitment
4.0   ORGANIZATION
    4.1   Conceptualization of a value
    4.2   Organization of a value system
5.0   CHARACTERIZATION BY A VALUE OR VALUE COMPLEX
    5.1   Generalized set
    5.2   Characterization

Fig. 5   Summary of the Affective Domain

It has been argued that the evaluation component of the curriculum – the second area of the operational model which is being described – and the objectives component are interdependent since without knowing what we are supposed to be assessing, we can hardly make assessments. Through evaluation, more rational decisions might be made about the extent to which precisely-defined objectives have been, or can be, attained. But we have not behaved in this way. Indeed, it seems to be a characteristic of Man that he evaluates, judges or appraises almost everything which comes his way, but the criteria which he uses for his evaluations, judgments and appraisals are often highly egocentric.[15] It is easier to form opinions than to make judgments. Curriculum developers have not been exceptional in this respect. We are not clear yet about what we can do, or should try to do, with the potentially powerful techniques of evaluation.

If the objectives of a course have been identified and described in concise operational terms, it is logically a simple exercise to identify those aspects of a course which it is desirable to evaluate and then to choose an appropriate instrument or technique for each job. It is likely that information would be sought about the feasibility of the objectives; about the suitability of the content and the methods by which it is taught; about the pupils' needs and their achievements; and about the effectiveness of teacher preparation, before and during service.

A number of standard evaluation instruments are already available which might be modified to enable this information to be collected. Apart from traditional objective-type and essay-type tests, there are attitude scales, interest inventories, interviews, multiple assessments, survey techniques, and group observation methods. It will be more usual, however, for the teacher or evaluation unit to find that it is necessary to devise a special instrument for the assessment of a particular aspect of the new curriculum. Few teachers have the necessary skill to construct appropriate instruments of measurement, and training courses are urgently needed. Otherwise, the application of measurement techniques to curriculum development in this country will continue to be confined largely to the conventional examination of individual gains in terms of simple cognitive end-products. We are not concerned in curriculum evaluation with selecting or ranking individuals but with overall changes in group performance. For this purpose, the evaluation instruments do not need to be as refined as tests for discriminating between individuals, although account still needs to be taken of the principles of test construction such as the validity of the instrument, its reliability and sensitivity. Curriculum evaluation is an integral component of the curriculum which we have not utilized adequately. If the techniques were developed, it would enable us to make a more scientific attack on the problem of curriculum renewal.

Turning now to the knowledge component of the curriculum, the prime question posed by the model is: how can the curriculum content be selected and organized so that the objectives of the school are most likely to be attained? We are agreed that the school's responsibility extends beyond the teaching of artificially circumscribed packages of information. The knowledge component is synthesized from the disciplines. The disciplines are the raw material by means of which we expect to achieve our stated objectives. They are the resource from which appropriate experiences arise for the education of children and adults. One of the most significant contemporary developments in curriculum study at school level has been the re-examination of the disciplines as sources for learning. More attention is being given in curriculum building to the basic concepts and methods of enquiry which are used by scientists, by mathematicians, by historians and so on. Our understanding of knowledge depends on the concepts we invent, such as force in physics, the bond in chemistry, scarcity in economics and style in literature; and the broader organizing principles that we find, for example, in the early years of the Nuffield Foundation chemistry course – mass relationship among reacting substances, energy in chemical reactions, and the importance of structure. In this new chemistry course, two alternative schemes are proposed through which an understanding of the same broad principles might be gained. The factual information in the two schemes differs significantly. By drawing attention to the fundamental structures of the disciplines in school work – not, of course, by direct teaching but through deliberately contrived learning experiences – the possibility of transfer is increased; that is, application to other situations of the principles and concepts which characterize a discipline are more likely. Another reason for a greater emphasis on structure is that it could bring elementary and advanced knowledge into a closer relationship since the sequence and relevance of fundamental ideas would be more carefully worked out. The selection of characteristic principles and concepts in any particular discipline and the arrangement of them in sequential and logical order is too big a job for one person. It is a task for a team which should include university specialists and other consultants as well as teachers. If school work is to become more relevant and remain relevant to the rapidly growing bodies of knowledge and to the increasingly complex society in which we live, we should no longer expect individuals to write syllabuses and text books. It is a foolish builder who does not take advice before he lays the foundations for his building. Teachers are builders and they cannot be expected to keep in touch with what is going on at the rock face of knowledge. Having designed a new course, the team of teachers and specialists should keep it under review to ensure that it continues to reflect the changing nature of the discipline. In the curriculum projects developed in this country during recent years, groups of people have been responsible in each case for the knowledge components of the courses. There has been some uneasiness on the part of a few teachers about the apparent loss of freedom to teach what they want to teach. Perhaps the professional autonomy of teachers should rest more on the freedom to decide how to teach rather than what to teach.

An unfortunate result of contemporary curriculum developments, even in the junior schools, has been to focus attention on individual disciplines without concern for their relationships to other fields and to neglect the overall structure of the whole school programme. We need to consider the types of relationships that should obtain both *within* and *between* the main areas of knowledge. Essentially, problems of relationships are problems of classification (on which there is a growing literature). The theory of knowledge raises many questions about the relationship of the various disciplines to the development of mind and to the nature of knowledge. For the purposes of understanding relationships between disciplines in curriculum study, two views of the nature of knowledge are helpful.

First, it is generally recognized that the natural sciences, mathematics, the humanities and the social sciences are four distinct groupings of organized disciplines, each of which uses key concepts and methods to view the environment in a different way. But, with the possible exception of mathematics, curriculum workers are giving little attention to these recognized broad groups. As already stated, attention tends to be directed to individual disciplines. In the Nuffield Foundation Science Teaching O-level Project, physicists, chemists and biologists have gone their way largely independent of each other. If we are to organize curriculum content for the purpose of attaining well-defined objectives and, in particular, to give experience of the unique concepts and methods used in each area of learning, the isolation of separate disciplines at school level should, it is suggested, be questioned. A gradual shift to broader groupings of knowledge seems desirable. Perhaps the four groupings of disciplines could furnish a framework for a planned programme of general education which would give the child adequate experience of all the ways of knowing and doing, and which would avoid inefficient repetition of a limited range of kinds of experience. Our treatment in schools during the 1940s and 1950s of general science and social studies has taught us to be cautious about grouping disciplines together. Certainly, during the general science movement we were more concerned with the informational content of courses than with underlying concepts and methods of enquiry. Teachers were not adequately prepared for the change through in-service courses and continued to think and teach in terms of biological, chemical and physical topics. The textbooks and the examination papers continued to reflect sharply the separate disciplines. The lesson is that unified courses must evolve slowly out of those principles and methods from the separate disciplines which are interrelated and fundamental. A willingness on the part of subject specialists to search for new patterns of knowledge for use in the curriculum might provide a greater measure of coherence and relatedness for the curriculum as a whole.

Consideration of the kind of integration which should be aimed at in curriculum-building *between* the broad areas of knowledge, rather than *within* each area, is helped by a second view of the nature of knowledge which relates the disciplines to specific modes of thinking or kinds of cognitive operation.

Peterson[16] urges us to stop thinking of general education in secondary schools in terms of general knowledge, but rather in terms of the development of four main modes of thought: the analytic, the empirical, the moral, and the aesthetic. Phenix[17] proposes six realms of meaning in his generic classification of knowledge: symbolics, empirics, aesthetics, ethics, synoptics, and synnoetics (a term used by Phenix to represent personal or relational knowledge as in certain aspects of philosophy). (See Fig. 6.) Disciplines are rarely assignable to a single mode of thought or realm of meaning: for example, literature contributes to the development of both moral and aesthetic judgments.

REALMS OF MEANING	DISCIPLINES
Symbolics	Ordinary language, mathematics
Empirics	Physical sciences, social sciences
Aesthetics	Music, visual arts, literature
Ethics	Moral philosophy
Synoptics	History, religion
Synnoetics	Philosophy, psychology

Fig. 6 Classification of Knowledge

This view of the heterogeneous character of knowledge needs to be taken into account when building the curriculum if the child is to experience all the ways of thinking appropriate to his level of attainment and to his environment. There is little evidence that there is one universal method to deal with problems in all fields, as Dewey's problem-solving approach seemed to suggest; or that there is a recognizable unity in knowledge which when found will close Snow's gap. Indeed, as we have seen, the trend today is towards a multitude of methods and conceptual schemes. The view of the nature of knowledge which relates different disciplines to specific modes of thought or meaning seems to suggest that an appropriate relationship in the curriculum between the broad areas of knowledge would be that which resulted in the exercise of *all* modes of thought at a level appropriate to the learner.

Apart from integration within and between areas of know-

ledge, there are two further criteria which the teacher uses for
the effective construction of the knowledge component of a
curriculum. These are reiteration, and sequence of elements of
the courses. 'Reiteration' refers to the repetition of major curriculum elements. For example, the fundamental concept of
energy in science must recur again and again at many points in
a course. 'Sequence' is related to reiteration, but sequence, as a
criterion for curriculum building, emphasizes that each successive experience – relating to energy, for example – should
build upon the preceding one. Reiteration, sequence and
integration are guiding principles for the teacher in the detailed
organization of an effective course.

Paul Hirst[18] has warned us that 'decisions about the content
of courses cannot be taken without careful regard to the
abilities and interests of the students for whom they are
designed'. What learning experiences can be provided *through*
the organized content of the curriculum that are likely to result
in the attainment of the teacher's objectives? This is the last
major curriculum component, 'Learning Experiences'.

The term 'learning experiences' is intended to refer to the
interaction between the learner and the external factors in the
environment to which he is exposed and can react. When we
are referring to the curriculum model, learning experiences
must be restricted, by definition, to those which are 'planned
and guided by the school', including societal opportunities
arranged by the school, the nature of the school community,
the relationships between pupils and teachers, variations arising
from individual differences and levels of readiness, the actual
content of each lesson and the methods by which it is presented
to the child. This is the area of curriculum to which most
attention is given in the day-by-day work of the school and
during courses for student teachers and teachers. The other
curriculum areas tend to be set aside. The general principle that
a pupil learns through what he does or experiences is emphasized and, if these experiences are appropriate and within
the capacity of the pupil, the objectives may be attained. In
teacher-training we are concerned with the process of plan-

ning the learning experiences to achieve particular aims. To guide us in this planning, ideas have been freely borrowed from other disciplines, particularly from psychology and sociology. Although these disciplines do not pretend to speak with one voice about any aspect of human learning or behaviour, educators have tended to use selected findings for prescriptive purposes. Professor Simon[19] dealt with this problem in his inaugural lecture (November 1966) when he reminded us that 'some of the worst mistakes [in education] have followed from transferring techniques and concepts uncritically from one province to another'. Two American curriculum theorists[20] wrote recently that the application of psychology, sociology and anthropology to practical considerations of schooling 'magnifies their normal limitations and clouds the dialogue on curriculum'. There has been a tendency to pick out findings which seem to support one's own opinions with the result that extreme positions acquire apparent support. The study of curriculum, along the lines which arc being proposed, holds out some hope for the 'fruitful co-operation' with other disciplines about which Professor Simon spoke.

The curriculum model steers the selection of learning experiences towards precisely defined ends so that the curriculum builder is in a position to consult the psychologist or the sociologist about quite specific questions. For example, recent work suggests that a child's experience is at least as important as maturation in determining his readiness for certain kinds of learning. If this is so, it would be feasible to plan the experiences that children have through the curriculum to achieve, say, a faster rate of development. In a particular area of the curriculum, such as scientific activities with junior school children, psychologists might look at the question of the optimum age at which children are capable of carrying out certain kinds of problem-solving activities. Empirical classroom-based curriculum studies offer the possibility of more fruitful co-operation with allied disciplines.

Another example of possible co-operation at the operational level relates to the new technology of learning – team teaching, television, language laboratories, programmed learning and other innovations. Many specific problems[21] face teachers who are beginning to use these instructional media. Which combination of resources is appropriate for teaching a particular topic to achieve a named purpose with a given group of children? In view of the changing theories about individual differences, how can we reconcile the development of mass instruction through television with the technology associated with individualized instruction, such as teaching machines? How does one medium interact with other media? How do these media interact with different types of pupils and teachers?

It must be acknowledged again that the completed model which has been presented inevitably results in a Procrustean view of the curriculum. But the model makes some theoretical formulation and empirical study of curriculum matters possible and limits the occasions when a crude pragmatic approach has to be used. It also promotes an interactive relationship between educational theory and classroom practice, and checks the false separation of theory from practice about which teachers and student teachers, with justification, complain. Assuming this model for the curriculum has some validity, what are its implications, particularly for the education of teachers both before service and during service? The remainder of this paper is concerned with the implications of the curriculum theory model which has been outlined.

There seems to be an overriding need for a drastic change of policy towards many curriculum matters. If the trial-and-error methods, which individual teachers at present practise within a framework of control from outside the classroom, are to be replaced by a system based on co-operative effort and objective evaluation, then there must be a willingness on the part of everyone concerned to participate actively in the curriculum building process and to try out the programmes which by co-operative effort have been produced. Many teachers are discouraged by their efforts to influence the direction of curriculum change. They feel thwarted by a policy which in their view leaves insufficient authority in their hands. Does the professional relationship between teachers, headteachers, administrators and central authority inhibit curriculum development in any way? Enquiry suggests that teacher involvement in curriculum projects might be encouraged and made more efficient by some shifts in the power structure, in the distribution of economic and human resources, and in the management of policy.

A second change is implied, particularly for the secondary school and higher education, by what has been said about the autonomy and diversity of the various disciplines of knowledge. This view of knowledge exposes vast areas of many syllabuses of work which are useless and outdated and which overlap in educational purpose. For reasons given earlier, a more central position for knowledge in curriculum planning is claimed. There are no signs in curriculum studies, either in England or elsewhere, as far as I know, of detailed attention being given to the integration of the curriculum as a whole. Curriculum projects deal usually with single subjects. The implication of the view expressed about the nature of knowledge is that we should be moving cautiously from patterns of single subject study to grouped disciplines. Professor Neustadt[22] and Professor Grodecki[23] each referred in their inaugural lectures to the same integrative problem in relation to the teaching in universities of sociology and law.

But the message arising from the proposed rationale for curriculum construction which rings louder and clearer than any other is that the reform of the curriculum will not come about without the total involvement of teachers. How can this be achieved? How are conditions to be created for the necessary involvement? We have started to develop a new concept of in-service education for teachers in the School of Education at Leicester, but, before I refer to it, let us first look at the national picture.

It is becoming manifest that the projects for curriculum renewal which have been introduced during the past five years by the Nuffield Foundation and the Schools Council are not passing phenomena but indicate what will become the accepted

pattern for building new curricula. During the trial stages of a
project, the pre-training of those teachers who are participating
in the trials can be centrally organized. But when the new
materials become generally available – as happened last sum-
mer with the Nuffield O-level science books, specially designed
apparatus and audio-visual materials – the demand from
teachers for re-training courses cannot be met from existing
resources, either centrally or locally. The Department of
Education and Science spent only £18,000 on short courses
during 1963–64. During 1966–67, it was proposed to spend
£100,000.[24] Although this is a notable increase, it is only
6s. 8d. per teacher per annum, or £14 over the whole of his
working life. Services provided locally by the universities, local
education authorities and professional associations have also
been stepped up, but the re-training of all the teachers who
wish to use each newly completed curriculum project is already
beyond our existing means. At the present time, the potential
market for courses in primary mathematics and also in primary
science exceeds 100,000 teachers, and tens of thousands of
secondary school science teachers are eager for the opportunity to discuss the interpretation and use of the new Nuffield
courses. Furthermore, in many cases a single short course is not
likely to bring about the degree of modification in teaching
methods which is desired. Radical changes based on a new set
of objectives are often proposed. Unless the teacher is given
support over a period of time, he may just move towards a
superficial appearance of change. In the C. D. Butler Memorial
Lecture at Exeter in October 1966, Robert Morris[25] warned
us about the danger in the changeover to comprehensive
education of being 'lulled into a state of damaging complacency
about the rectitude of the system without being concerned
about its purposes'. It is so with each new curriculum programme. Real reform can only be achieved, in my view,
through a full measure of teacher involvement.

The road to this kind of involvement seems to be, first, to
interest the teachers in a particular line of development – not
usually difficult; then to bring teachers together in circum-

stances which will create a willingness to enter with confidence into a commitment to work as a member of a curriculum group; and finally to arrange for the provision of all the resources and specialist help for which the group asks. The conventional method of in-service provision through conferences and short courses of lectures rarely provides all three conditions for total involvement – interest, commitment and resources. There is no doubt that the short series of lectures is an effective way of keeping the teaching profession informed and interested about changes in educational theory and practice, but there is evidence that it is not an effective method of bringing about desirable changes in the classroom. For this purpose, teachers' centres are proving to be effective instruments of change. The concept of a teachers' centre, such as we are trying to develop at Leicester, is a deliberate attempt to involve teachers in their own curriculum problems and development. At the present time, twelve different groups of teachers are provided with some of the resources they need, including specialist guidance largely from my colleagues on the staff of the School of Education. Most of these study groups are using the curriculum model which I have outlined as a design for solving the curriculum task each group has set itself. The creative consequences are, I think, most encouraging. The local education authorities in the area are beginning to make provisions for their own teachers' centres and, if this trend develops, the School of Education might appropriately assume the role of consultant and co-ordinator in the area. We might also help to train the leaders of curriculum groups in the principles and techniques of curriculum construction and evaluation. Not the least of our rôles must be to continue with operational research, particularly in the area of curriculum evaluation which we have made our special concern. Curriculum development and research work along the lines indicated cannot proceed without the full co-operation of teachers and local education authorities.

Two further implications of the curriculum theory model should be mentioned briefly – its significance for the preservice training of teachers and for the dynamics of curriculum change.

Although we are aware that it is not desirable to separate theory from practice in the initial training of teachers, we fall too often into the trap of dealing with a part of curriculum study, which we call 'method' work, as though it was a separate entity from selected aspects of educational psychology, philosophy, sociology and history, which we call 'theory'. A model for the curriculum could have a co-ordinating function. If the educational objectives of College of Education or University teacher-training courses were set out in operational terms – and the difficulties of this exercise have been stressed – it would become feasible to ask more precise questions about the knowledge component of the education course and about relevant learning experiences. These questions could well act as new foci for the selection of the most relevant concepts, principles and theories from the appropriate disciplines. Perhaps the material dealt with would not differ greatly from the content of education as we know it, but the emphases would certainly be different and much material would be discarded. Educationists would then be in a position to consult specialists in the disciplines allied to education for advice about particular problems in the same way as the medical profession calls upon physiologists, biochemists, bacteriologists and so on.

And, finally, the last implication of this approach to the study of curriculum relates to the need for consideration of the implementation of the changes suggested. The manner in which dominant forces of the day have shaped the curriculum of the past is challenged. Although the influence of historical tradition, political expediency, economic priorities and social prejudice cannot wholly be eliminated – and it is not suggested that they should be – the theoretical model for the curriculum which has been put forward suggests the possibility that change can be effectively planned and predetermined on educational grounds. There is need to explore the nature of this planned collaborative process which involves relationships between teachers and curriculum specialists as well as between teachers and pupils. There is need for more adequate agencies for change, such as teachers' centres and a national evaluation service along the lines of the Educational Testing Service at Princeton, New Jersey. There is urgent need for research work into these matters if the dynamics of change in the curriculum development process are to be understood and, to some extent, controlled. There is *no* need to polarize the argument between planners and non-planners. A compromise is envisaged between planned decision-making and free choice as a result of more and better theory, and more and better research.

Some of the changes proposed will require a revolution in attitudes and methods related to curriculum development. That the revolution has started, there is no doubt. The goal is to plan and guide more of the child's experiences – not all – on the basis of a conceptual framework which is at least partly susceptible to theoretical study.

References

1 For example, the *Reports of the Science and Education Committee of the Science Masters' Association*, John Murray, 1961.
2 *Review of Educational Research*, vol. XXXVI, No. 3, June 1966, p. 341.
3 E. S. Maccia, 'Curriculum Theory and Policy', *Occasional Paper 65-176*, Educational Theory Center, Ohio State University.
4 G. A. Beauchamp, *Curriculum Theory*, Kegg Press, Wilmette, Illinois, 1961, p. 34.
5 Modified from V. E. Herrick and R. W. Tyler (editors), *Toward Improved Curriculum Theory*, Chicago University Press, 1950, p. 59.
6 E. S. Maccia, *Methodological Considerations in Curriculum Theory Building*, presented to A.S.C.D. Commission on Curriculum Theory, Chicago, 1965. In the brief statement about Maccia's work, I have used her form of words in places to retain the precision of her writing, but much of the carefully reasoned analysis is omitted. The original papers should be consulted to ensure a full understanding of the work.
7 E. S. Maccia, *Occasional Paper 65-176*, op. cit., p. 11.
8 P. B. Medawar, 'Is the Scientific Paper Fraudulent?' *Saturday Review*, 1 August 1964, pp. 42-3.
9 A. Miel, 'Reassessment of the Curriculum – Why?' in *A Reassessment of the Curriculum*, edited by D. Huebner, Bureau of Publications, Columbia University, New York, 1964, p. 20.

10 E. S. Maccia, *Methodological Considerations in Curriculum Theory Building*, op. cit., p. 7. It is suggested that 'model of' and 'theory' could be synonymous terms, but 'model for' cannot be more than theory models to develop theory.

11 G. H. Bantock, *The Implications of Literacy*, Leicester University Press, 1966, p. 16.

12 *Educational Research Bulletin XIII*, No. 8, 1933, pp. 196–206.

13 B. S. Bloom, et al. (editors), *Taxonomy of Educational Objectives: Handbook I, The Cognitive Domain*, Longmans Green, 1956; and D. R. Krathwohl, B. S. Bloom, and B. B. Masia. *Taxonomy of Educational Objectives: Handbook II, The Affective Domain*, Longmans Green, 1964.

14 Ibid., *II*, p. 29.

15 Ibid., *I*, p. 185.

16 A. D. C. Peterson, *Arts and Science Sides in the Sixth Form*, Oxford University Department of Education, 1960.

17 P. H. Phenix, *Realms of Meaning*, McGraw-Hill, New York, 1964, p. 28.

18 P. H. Hirst, 'Liberal Education and the Nature of Knowledge', in *Philosophical Analysis and Education*, edited by R. D. Archambault, Routledge and Kegan Paul, 1965, p. 135.

19 B. Simon, *Education: The New Perspective*, Leicester University Press, 1967.

20 A. R. King and J. A. Brownell, *The Curriculum and the Disciplines of Knowledge*, John Wiley, New York, 1966, p. 109.

21 *Review of Educational Research*, vol. XXXVI, No. 3, June 1966, ch. 4.

22 I. Neustadt, *Teaching Sociology*, Leicester University Press, 1965, pp. 15–18.

23 J. K. Grodecki, *Legal Education: Dilemmas and Opportunities*, Leicester University Press, 1967.

24 R. Morris, *The In-service Education of Teachers*, Exeter University Institute of Education, 1966, p. 6.

25 Ibid., p. 9.

PAPER 2

The Contribution of Philosophy to the Study of the Curriculum

Paul H. Hirst

IT is slowly becoming less necessary for anyone talking about the significance of philosophy for education to launch first into an account of the nature of philosophy as understood by contemporary professionals. I must, however, say one or two things on this subject so that it is quite clear how I at least see my brief.

Philosophy, I shall take it, is above all concerned with clarification of the concepts and propositions in which our experience and activities are intelligible. It is interested in answering questions about the meaning of terms and expressions, about the logical relations and the presuppositions these terms and expressions involve. As I shall regard it, philosophy is not a speculative super-science that tries to answer questions about some ultimate reality; it is not the pursuit of moral knowledge; it is not the great integrator of all human understanding into a unified view of man, God and the Universe; it is not a science – as is, for instance, psychology or sociology – concerned to understand what is the case in terms of experiment and observation. It is rather a distinctive type of higher order pursuit, an analytical pursuit, with the ambition of understanding the concepts used in all other forms of lower order knowledge and awareness. Philosophy, as I see it, is a second order area of knowledge, concerned above all with the necessary features of our primary forms of understanding and awareness in the sciences, in morals, in history and the like. Although expressed this way philosophical understanding sounds abstract and remote from other concerns, it can, nevertheless, be of enormous importance in mundane affairs; for without a self-conscious and critical use of the concepts employed every day in making judgments, in deciding to do this rather than that, one can easily lapse into very serious errors of judgment, both theoretical and practical. In much of what I have to say I hope to show just this relevance for philosophical concern with the concepts and propositions in which our knowledge and judgments are cast. I therefore take it as my brief to try to show where clarifications of a conceptual kind can contribute to responsible and rational curriculum development.

At first sight it might seem appropriate for me to begin my paper with an analysis of the meaning of the term 'curriculum'. Certainly I must say something on this score. But the philosopher of education must recognize that just as too little analysis of a concept can lead to distortion in judgments and understanding which employ it, so too much analysis can deflect attention from the actual concerns and practical judgments which he wishes to illuminate. I am, therefore, going to content myself with enough general comment on what is meant by the curriculum as is relevant to practical problems and will put in context the other things I want to say.

The term curriculum is, of course, excessively broad, and I shall take it to mean a programme of activities designed so that pupils will attain, as far as possible, certain educational ends or objectives. I do not wish to imply by this that a curriculum must be a programme or sequence of activities that is not to be changed in any respect by the pupils, that it must be completely determined by teachers. Nor do I wish to imply that curriculum activities are teachers' activities as distinct from the activities of pupils. We are concerned, of course, with both. Activities on the part of the child are essential if there is to be any significant learning at all, and activities on the part of the teacher are necessary to produce the learning with which education is concerned.

What I want to bring out, in making this very brief statement as to how I understand the term curriculum, are the three elements that seem to be implied in the very notion of a curriculum and which are therefore essential features in rational curriculum planning. No doubt the other contributors to this series refer to the same three elements, as their significance now seems generally agreed.

First, there can be no curriculum without educational objectives. Unless there is some point to planning the activities, some intended educational outcome, however vague this might be, there is no such thing as a curriculum. What is more, it is educational objectives with which we are concerned, and that means the objectives, to which the curriculum is the means, are objectives which satisfy certain criteria for education. I shall, for my purposes, assume the criteria that Professor Peters has recently elucidated. That is, I shall take it that in education we are concerned with pupils coming to participate in the forms of awareness and the pursuits of some worthwhile form of life.[1]

But if a curriculum is a plan of activities aimed at achieving objectives, it is a plan involving two other elements, a content to be used and methods to be employed to bring about learning. By content is usually meant the particular plays of Shakespeare that are studied, the particular elements of history considered – say, the foreign policy of Great Britain in 1914 – the particular social or moral problems that are discussed, and the like. And by methods, or learning experiences, we usually mean the discussions or lecture techniques used, the experiments done, the surveys conducted, the demonstrations given, the acting pupils do, and so on. Although we must obviously keep distinct the content of the curriculum and the methods employed, I think this distinction is for some purposes rather artificial, for the content used sometimes closely depends on the sort of methods employed and vice versa. For my purposes it is important to keep clearly distinct the content and the methods, for changes in the one do not necessarily demand a revolution in the other. Clearly, granted certain objectives and methods, one can in many cases change the content that is used to achieve these. If one is after certain forms of aesthetic appreciation, one can use Play A rather than Play B, Poem C rather than Poem D. Equally, given certain objectives and a specific content, one can vary the actual methods employed. One can then, to some extent, consider content and method independently, given a set of objectives, even if it is too simple to regard them in stark isolation. The intricacies of their inter-relation I cannot go into here.

What I should like to stress now is that for curriculum planning to be rational, it must start with clear and specific objectives, and then, and only then, address itself to discovering the plan of means, the content and methods, in terms of which these objectives are to be obtained. It is a simple logical nonsense to pretend that a series of activities form a curriculum, or a part of a curriculum, if they are not responsibly designed to obtain specifiable objectives. The use of free activity periods by the inexperienced and unthoughtful forms an obvious case in point here. There is no reason whatever to suppose that free activity will necessarily be educational, even if it occurs in a well-equipped environment. It is, I think, pure deception to regard such activity as part of a curriculum if it is not structured to obtain educational objectives. If one redefines what is meant by a curriculum to include this sort of random pursuit, that is to win only a verbal battle. It remains logically the case that these activities are not designed to achieve educational ends, and whether any education in fact occurs is purely fortuitous. It seems to me just nonsense to pretend that these pursuits really form part of what is responsibly known as a curriculum.

Having made this point about the necessity of rational curriculum planning beginning with objectives, I must add that I think it important not to confuse either methods or content with objectives, or to regard these as somehow having a right to determine educational objectives. Take a term like 'problem solving'. It is common nowadays to think of the ability to solve problems as a principal educational end. Problem solving may, of course, also be an important method for attaining other educational objectives. But to assert that this is an educational end is simply to put up one possible objective to be considered along with many others. As a means, it is again only one among many possibilities and may have limited value. But we must not run from the claim that it is an effective means to the claim that it is thereby an important end. In the same way we must never take the content of the curriculum as specifying the objectives. In a great deal of formal education, the kind that many of us deplore, I think this is exactly what happens. The content of the curriculum, the works of Shakespeare or the areas of science and mathematics that are to be used as means for achieving very complex and sophisticated educational ends, is often taken as itself providing the educational objectives. The result is that the education concerned becomes directed towards the mastery of a particular content of propositions, when the propositions in this particular area of knowledge should be employed as a means of achieving very complex objectives by way of particular dispositions, types of intellectual skills, various habits of mind and the like.

Having made these points by way of a long introduction, I want to turn now to the particular areas where philosophical work can, I think, help curriculum planning. It can, I think, help in at least the following four ways. There are others, but I am not going to consider them in this paper.

First, it can help us to understand the nature of educational objectives, what kind of achievements we are after.

Secondly, it can help us to understand the structure, or the inter-relatedness, of the objectives.

Thirdly, it can contribute to our grasp of the nature of curriculum activities.

Fourthly, it can contribute to our understanding of the structure of curriculum plans which, it seems to me, are dependent on both the content and the methods which we wish to employ .

Let me turn first then to the nature of educational objectives. What are the objectives that we are after? What kinds of things constitute the end achievements of education for which the curriculum is the means? Clearly they are developments of individual people. They are achievements brought about by learning rather than by maturation, and we characteristically list them as achievements of knowledge, belief, values, habits, attitudes and the like. But what is the range of these achievements, and what are their distinct categories? What exactly is meant by having knowledge? What do we mean by a skill? What is a fact? What is a value? These questions, it seems to me, are philosophical in character, and a clearer grasp of the answers to them could contribute a great deal to more intelligent educational planning.

B. S. Bloom and his colleagues have in recent years produced two instalments of a now celebrated classification of educational objectives.[2] They divide the area into three domains, the cognitive, the affective, and the psycho-motor. In the cognitive domain they list first such objectives as a knowledge of specifics – meaning by this, of particular items of information, a knowledge of terminology, of conventions, of classifications, of methodologies, of principles and generalizations, of theories. They then classify intellectual abilities and skills, dividing these into such groups as the skills and abilities connected with comprehension, translation, application, the analysis and breaking down into elements of communications that we receive, synthesizing communications and evaluating them.

In the same way there is an attempt to classify the objectives we are after in the affective domain. First there are objectives connected with attending to phenomena, from awareness to controlled selection. There follow groupings of dispositions to respond, from mere acquiescence to enjoyment. Similarly in matters of valuing, organizing and the formation of a whole complex of values.

Bloom has endeavoured to setout a framework of categories in which we can clearly distinguish educational objectives. This, I think, has enormous value. To begin with, it brings out the tremendous diversity of the kinds of objectives we are after in education. We are not simply after people learning facts, not simply after their learning skills, not simply after their learning values or attitudes or habits. We are after all these things and more, and within any of these categories, with very diverse skills, attitudes and dispositions. Certainly to list objectives in these categories, provided we formulate them in great detail, is an extremely important exercise in planning a curriculum and is a very good antidote to pursuing the usual limited range of objectives of which we are most directly conscious when we think about school work. The classification too is concerned with intended changes in the behaviour of students which can be evaluated. By contrast, you are only too aware, I am sure, of the older type of objectives which people used to suggest, and still do, for the curriculum: the ability to solve problems, the ability to pursue enquiries, to take decisions for oneself, to think creatively, to be imaginative, to have critical thought. These global, general qualities of mind, attitudes, or whatever you like to call them, need to be analysed in great detail before they are practically significant objectives, and Bloom's taxonomy is a great help in this process.

But in spite of these advantages, the taxonomy is limited in its value, for it cannot of itself draw attention to the *nature* of the different classes of objectives listed or their complex inter-relations. We need to know what is involved in knowing facts, solving problems, applying knowledge and so on. Indeed we want to know what 'facts' are and what kinds there are of them.

Take this idea of a fact. If we spell out that we are going to teach children certain facts or specifics, let us see what this implies. Look at a simple fact, such as Harold Wilson is Prime Minister. If a child is to understand this fact, this item of knowledge, then to begin with he must understand what a Prime Minister is. He must also be able to identify Harold Wilson. What is more, if he is to learn this as a fact he must know that it is true, and he must have some idea of what difference it makes that Harold Wilson and not someone else is the Prime Minister. I would suggest therefore that it is quite impossible to learn facts, to know them as facts, without acquiring the basic concepts and the criteria for truth involved. Now that is to suggest that the notion of a fact is not a logically primitive educational objective. It presupposes certain other more fundamental objectives so that without the pursuit of these, possibly in the same context, one cannot teach facts. One might, of course, teach words, but that is not the point. In commenting on this I have given the beginnings of a simple analysis of what is meant by a fact. We usually think of facts, in our everyday context, as just lying about the world, somehow being registered by us as on sensitive plates. But of course the facts are always what you know to be the case, and, without certain concepts, you would fail to be aware of certain facts, even about the room in which you sit. The notion of a fact needs therefore to be spelt out with great care if we are to know what is involved in teaching facts. And one can go further, of course. I have said that one cannot have facts without concepts. But what is a concept? Is this a logically primitive element? Here is another philosophical question important for curriculum planning.

Or take another range of objectives altogether. What is an intellectual skill, for example, adding up in arithmetic, being able to count? What is this ability to deduce that we wish children to acquire? Unless we know what we mean by deduction or by counting, it seems to me that we may be using methods in our education which are not seriously, in a considered way, directed to the objectives. Deduction is a very good example here. Is to deduce something to have a piece of mental machinery ticking over in a certain way? Is a person who can deduce from A and B that C is the case somebody who has got a piece of psychological machinery 'tuned' to work effectively? Is the person who cannot deduce one who suffers from having a rusty piece of machinery instead? We usually think of deduction as a psychological process, but is it a sequence of events in the mind? Are there any actual psychological processes which are in fact necessary to deducing? The prime example of deduction is perhaps a mathematical theorem, so how do mathematicians work out theorems? Do

THE CONTRIBUTION OF PHILOSOPHY

they go down a ladder of reasoning, working strictly in a given order? Generally speaking, no mathematician does that. Frequently he starts from the bottom and works backwards, he shoots up a blind alley in the middle and fails to get anywhere, or thinks of a useful analogy. What the sequence of his thought is does not in fact matter, for his processes of thought are not the deduction; the deduction is the pattern of the end achievement that he establishes. To teach children to deduce is not to teach them to think along particular psychological channels, it is to teach them – whatever channels or psychological processes they use – to produce certain patterns of statements in the end. If one sees deducing as achieving certain public performances rather than as achieving an inner sequence of thought, one's objectives in this enterprise are of a quite different nature.

Or again, take something like the ability to solve problems. What is meant by this phrase? Obviously one begins by asking what problems: moral problems, scientific problems, mathematical problems? Clearly these are very different in nature. Can we assume that the ability to solve mathematical problems is the same as the ability to solve problems in morals? What is more, even to understand a scientific problem, as distinct from a moral problem, presupposes a great deal of scientific knowledge. It is only when one has done a lot of science that one can recognize scientific problems for what they are. And similarly, it is only when one has done a great deal of thinking about moral matters that one recognizes moral problems as different in kind from those of science, needing to be solved in a quite different manner. The notion, therefore, of developing an ability to solve problems is radically suspect in a way that cannot be revealed simply by a classification of objectives. What is more, one can only pursue the solving of particular types of problems if at the same time one is prepared to teach a very great deal of fact, a very large number of principles, of criteria and tests for truth. All of these must be employed in recognizing a problem for what it is, let alone solving it. One cannot therefore pursue the end of problem solving for one type of problem in isolation from pursuing other objectives, and one cannot, in pursuing the ability to solve scientific problems, assume one is thereby pursuing the ability to solve moral problems and historical problems as well. There are many general terms of this sort for objectives and I suggest that one of the fundamental tasks of the philosopher is to help people break all these down so that we know what is involved in trying to develop these abilities, attitudes and the like.

There is another way of expressing curriculum objectives which needs to be philosophically analysed and exposed. Certainly Bloom's taxonomy gets us away from this. It is the suggestion that we can usefully express the ends of the curriculum in such terms as promoting growth, pursuing felt interests, satisfying needs. These terms are again global in their intentions, and their content is totally unspecified. 'Growth' and 'need' can be used as educational objectives because they presuppose a set of in-built norms, in-built standards, and so indicate, however vaguely, something that is thought to be desirable. But talking about the pursuit of growth and the satisfacton of needs must not blind us to the need to formulate in detail what objectives constitute growth and what precisely it is that pupils need. The notion of growth itself, once taken out of its biological context, contains no clear indications as to what is to be aimed at. Take Dewey's old example: is pursuing burglary and developing a high art in this 'growth'? Well, obviously in an educational sense, no. But why not exactly? What developments, what objectives, do constitute growth? The term itself picks out no clear answer; we have to determine quite independently what content it shall have. If one turns to a term like 'needs', then one can certainly talk about basic needs which people may have of a biological or a psychological kind. But do these really spell out curriculum objectives for us? In what sense do children need arithmetic or need to solve practical problems? In what sense do they need to understand the science taught to them? Only in a highly conventionalized social sense. The norm or value that makes us think of these as needs is a social norm, not a 'natural' one. Saying what children need is only a cloaked way of saying what we judge they ought to have. Let us then remove the cloak and its suggestions that in nature we can find what children ought to have in terms of their growth and their needs. And let us accept the fact that we must plan and specify ourselves which educational objectives we are after.[3]

The idea that educational objectives can be spelt out in terms of interests can, I think, also be analysed away. The interests of children – if one takes the felt interests that they have – will never, in many cases, produce the educational objectives we want. What is more important is the assumption that interests, like needs, are naturally given and are not the product of social factors. But interests can be created, and it is surely a basic function of education to create interests in what is worthwhile. Once more we must realize that a global term cannot be the source of specific educational objectives. It just hides the fact that people are writing in their own judgments as to what objectives should be chosen. Such terms cannot give us specific educational objectives which can function as aims in the educational enterprise at a working level, for to be meaningful they presuppose a particular content of this kind.

[margin note: But see p. 30.]

In talking about the nature of objectives I have at times strayed over into saying things about the structure of objectives, and to this I now want to turn explicitly.

I have said that one cannot know facts independently of having the relevant concepts. Similarly one cannot have particular emotions, for example, envy, without making relevant judgments, in this case that things are of value. The whole possibility of the emotion of envy, therefore, presupposes that one can judge things to be of value. This is to imply that there is a complex interrelation of objectives here that must be recognized. Emotional development is intimately related with knowledge, beliefs, values. That objectives in general are not elements which can be considered in isolation, that they are necessarily intimately related to each other, and that some objectives are completely unattainable unless attention is paid to others which are logically prior to them, is a philosophical truth we have got to take much more seriously than we have done in the past.

The complex relations between the many different objectives that we might wish to pursue in education, between facts and skills, between particular types of facts, particular types of skills and so on, has not yet begun to be worked out in detail, and one of the things that I think must be said about Bloom's taxonomy, is that it gets us nowhere in understanding these complex inter-relationships. It may be a classification useful for many purposes. But what we need for fundamental curriculum planning is a scheme which goes much further, which will help us to map out how the attainment of objectives *a*, *b* and *c* is necessarily related to the attainment of objectives *d*, *e* and *f*.

Only in the area of propositional or theoretical knowledge has the question of the structure of objectives been at all systematically considered by philosophers, though there have been some attempts to deal with both emotions and skills.[4] I shall therefore confine myself to a recent attempt to map objectives in distinct areas of meaning and knowledge.

In his book *Realms of Meaning*, Professor Philip Phenix sets out a classification of the kinds of propositions and symbolic expressions that, in fact, we wish pupils to understand and to be able to employ.[5] He suggests that these fall into nine generic classes, as propositions can be seen to have three forms of extension or quantity and three forms of quality. As to quantity, propositions are either singular, relating to particulars only; or general, making a limited but general claim; or comprehensive, about a totality of some kind. As to intentional quality, there are statements of fact, of form and of norm. Statements of fact are of the kind, 'London is the capital of England', or 'Salt dissolves in water'. Statements of form are of a logical or formal nature, for example, 'Something cannot be both A and not A'. Statements of norm involve a standard or value, for example, 'You ought to tell the truth'. Here then are nine basic categories of propositions, or rather expressions, because Phenix includes, for instance, works of art as examples of propositions in this broad sense – those of singular fact, singular form, singular norm; general fact, general form, general norm; comprehensive fact, comprehensive form, comprehensive norm. Phenix sees these nine classes as together providing the distinguishing features of six fundamental realms of meaning that man has devised. It is in terms of these that man's conscious experience is defined and they are the foundation of all that is distinctively human. The task of general education is the handing on of these structured realms with their distinctive logics and forms of expression. The mapping of the features of the realms of meaning therefore provides a map of the central objectives of education, showing their differences and inter-relations.

The first thing to be said of Phenix's work is surely that he has attempted the central task of mapping objectives in a way quite beyond a mere classification, however useful that might be. The crucial questions of related elements of learning, of similarities and differences in meaning and in logical structure, are here examined. What is more, it seems to me that Phenix is right to begin the mapping by looking at different types of proposition, for there seem to be good grounds for taking these as primary elements of meaning. But why fasten on these features of propositions? Propositions could equally well be classified as, say, hypothetical and categorical, or analytic and synthetic. Why is it these do not give different realms of meaning? The answer is, I think, that types of meaning can only be classified along with types of claims to truth. Realms of meaning become distinct when we find different types of claims to knowledge, when there are principles by which we distinguish truth from error, right from wrong, beautiful from ugly, and so on. Certainly it seems to me one can classify propositions in the terms Phenix uses. But if we are to map out areas of distinct type of meaning, then his first categorization by quantity is surely rather irrelevant. It seems to me that there is nothing importantly different in type of meaning or knowledge between propositions which state singular facts, as distinct from those stating general or universal fact. Scientific meaning involves all these, for example. Much more to the point if one is concerned with classifying knowledge are the distinctions of his second kind between fact, form and norm. If one is to classify kinds of *true* propositions, and thus kinds of knowledge, one must do this, I think, by looking at what is necessary to such propositions. Kinds of meaning are, I think, related to kinds of test for truth or similar objective judgments, and therefore the central differences will be discerned by looking at variations in the type of tests for truth that we employ. This approach I have attempted elsewhere.[6]

I take it that propositions presuppose networks of concepts, as indeed Phenix does. I take it also that these are always connected with certain particular tests for truth. The crucial distinctions in meaning then are those between say, fact, form and norm, for these turn on types of tests for truth. One is concerned with the differences in the quality of propositions, though it seems to me Phenix has not gone far enough in disentangling the different kinds there are. I have argued that there are some six or seven types of 'quality', not merely three. What one is really saying here is that in the area of knowledge, of propositional knowledge, there are implicit interrelations of conceptual structures and tests for truth. As a result, learning what is the case, learning what is true in a particular area – science, say – or learning what ought to be the case in, say, morals, or learning what is claimed in the religious area, does involve the mastery of an interrelated body of concepts and certain tests for truth that go with these. In each case these are distinctive in kind and cannot in fact be equated with or reduced to concepts and tests of a type appropriate in some other area. This is to suggest that in any range of objectives of knowledge that we may set ourselves, there is an implicit structure of categories of objectives that are interrelated, and these are not simply optional interrelations. They are necessary interrelations implicit within the domain of knowledge itself.

Here then is a domain where philosophical work has at least begun mapping the relationship between some objectives. As yet very little has been done for any other range of objectives, seeking to outline the relationship between, say, different skills or attitudes, or these and propositional knowledge. Classification of this kind could, I am sure, help enormously in curriculum planning. Where specific problems have arisen in contemporary curricula there are now moves in this direction. Work is under way to clarify what is meant by moral education, what concepts there are involved here, how they differ from other concepts, what sort of judgments moral judgments are, what tests there are for moral propositions, what dispositions are necessary if people are actually to carry out the actions which they know to be right and good, and so on.[7] Something of the same sort does, I think, occur, though less self-consciously, when people re-plan curricula in science or mathematics in, for instance, the Nuffield or the Schools Council context. But the work is far more difficult than is often realized and it does seem to me that only good could come from employing in enterprises of this kind people whose job it is to analyse structures of concepts and their inter-relations.

I want now to pass to the third area where I think philosophers can help curriculum work. Granted a set of objectives, what of the nature of the means employed to attain these objectives? What of the activities that a curriculum plans? For instance, what do we mean by teaching, by learning, by instructing? How do these activities differ from indoctrinating, from conditioning, from brain-washing? Which of these activities are educational and why? These are typically philosophical questions about the meanings of terms. Take the term 'teaching'. What do we mean by teaching? Is it the label of a specific kind of activity, or is it in fact a label for a whole range of possible activities: explaining, demonstrating, film showing, asking questions, answering questions, lecturing? Teaching, I would suggest, is in fact not the label of a specific activity at all, for it is what is technically known as a poly-morphous concept. The activities it covers can take many different forms. But when is demonstrating something 'teaching', rather than just simply showing somebody what is the case? When does conversation become telling a person, and is telling teaching? What is it that makes these sub-activities into teaching rather than the carrying on of social intercourse of some other sort? When is showing a film part of teaching rather than entertainment? The answer is, I think, that teaching is the employment of these diverse activities with the deliberate intention of bringing about learning, and unless that is so, the activity, although it may be of the sort that could go on in teaching, cannot in these circumstances be described as such.[8]

But if teaching must be characterized as the intention to bring about learning, what is it to learn? Learning is, of course, something that pupils do, not teachers, but how are we to characterize this? Is learning one activity? Is learning a skill the same as learning a fact? Is learning a disposition the same thing as learning a habit? Is learning to carry out one's moral judgments the same sort of thing as learning to make the judgments? Manifestly the end states are quite different in learning to calculate, learning a fact, learning some particular sort of physical skill. And if the end achievements are so different, it is hardly likely that the activities of learning will be the same in all cases. One of the things that we have really got to get hold of is that if the objectives of education are as diverse as something like Bloom's taxonomy reveals, then the forms of learning activity that are appropriate will be as radically diverse. It is really quite absurd to imagine that one form of teaching, with a correlative form of learning, can be the instrument for the radically different ends we wish to achieve.

What the philosopher can try to do here is discover what the necessary conditions are for pupils achieving different sorts of objectives. What elements must occur in an activity if a pupil is to learn what we want him to learn? We can in fact start by looking at the achievement itself, analysing what is necessary to this, and then look for activities which will supply what is necessary. On the other hand, we can start by taking activities and, by analysing these, try to discover what it is logically possible for them to achieve.

Take the first approach. What is necessary to learning a concept like 'set' in mathematics? What is necessary to learning what is meant by 'devaluation' in economics? Is it necessary to be given the definition of 'set' in order to learn what is meant by it? Or do I have to be given some particular examples of 'sets' so that I can recognize what sort of things this definition covers? Have I then got the concept of 'set', or for that do I have to discover how to use the term in some mathematical context? If all I need is the definition, then all that is necessary is that I be told it, presupposing that I understand the terms used. If, however, what is wanted is that I should understand what lies underneath this, I shall need to be shown particular instances of 'sets'. If, however, what I am to attain is the full use of this concept in solving mathematical problems, then of course I shall have to be given practice in the deployment of it. Just to be told the definition could not result in my learning how to use the concept in this way. We have to get clear precisely what it is we wish to be learnt, what is necessary to it, and therefore what sort of activities must take place if the appropriate learning is to occur.

But we can in fact also approach the matter of learning and teaching the other way round, by looking at different activities. We can ask what we mean by 'learning by discovery', and what exactly could be learnt by discovery. Manifestly, there are many things a child could never learn by discovery; he must be told them if he is ever going to know them, unless by discovery you mean simply looking them up in a book. (And why exactly should he look them up in a book rather than be told them?) Similarly we can ask: what is play? What is learnt in problem solving? What can be learnt through dance and movement? Until we know the answers to these questions we are often using methods to teach we know not what. Forms of learning need to be related to the forms of achievement that we want. Philosophical analysis can, I think, help us get clearer, not only about the forms of achievement we want, that I talked about earlier, but about the activities of learning that are possible here. What type of activity can be used to teach what, that is the vital question.

I have framed questions throughout here, for although work has begun in this area, there is still a great deal of confusion which has to be cleared up. It is surprising how often people still assume that one type of formal activity can in fact bring about the radically diverse types of educational achievement that we nowadays expect schools to pursue. But, on the other hand, there is an alarming and ill-considered dogmatism in some quarters that uncritically rejects older methods and claims virtues for newer activities that by the nature of the case they could not possibly possess. If one wants a grasp of certain concepts, of certain skills, of certain habits, if one wants certain forms of information and so on, there are only *some* activities which can bring about these end products. There are certain activities which certainly could not, logically could not, result in the desired learning. What we need to do is to disentangle the various cases.

One last point in this connection. I have suggested that teaching is in fact the use of varied activities of many kinds to bring about learning. That is still far too general a description for what we want in schools. There are some methods which teachers should not use although they may bring about learning. Brain-washing may be a case in point. Indoctrination, which may use highly sophisticated and rational-seeming techniques, may be another. The reasons why these are ruled out of education are, I think, either moral or because the objectives pursued are not in fact in the end educationally acceptable. An indoctrinator may in fact indoctrinate a perfectly true piece of information and to that extent would seem to be using an educational procedure. But if it is indoctrination he uses, the methods, whatever they may be, are also aimed at other objectives which are anti-educational in that they are denying the development of a rational understanding of what is being communicated. We need therefore to review our methods in education, and in particular in moral and religious education, not only to see that the methods we employ are directed to objectives we do want, but to see that they are not also, at the same time, making it impossible to achieve other objectives we wish to pursue.[9]

Finally, what of the organization of the curriculum and the structuring of its sub-units? I spoke earlier of the structure of our objectives, and I want first to make clear one very important point. Whatever structures there may be within the domain of educational objectives, however cohesive and logically united a discipline such as, say, history may be, so that the elements of knowledge we wish acquired, the concepts, the facts, the principles, are all interrelated in some unified way, it does not follow necessarily that the curriculum should be organized into units of this kind. Nothing logically follows, necessarily, from the structure of the objectives of the curriculum to the structure of the means. Let me illustrate the point. A jigsaw puzzle may consist of domains of diverse colours, columns if you like, and across these may be traced shapes of one kind or another. Because the jigsaw puzzle necessarily involves piecing together coloured columns, does one *have* to do the jigsaw by directly paying attention to these coloured columns? Must one build it by first doing the red, then doing the blue, then doing the gold? Or by doing first a part of the red, then a part of the gold, then a part of the blue? Or can one not in fact forget the blue, red and gold and do the jigsaw puzzle by the patterns that are traced out across the colours? The answer is manifestly that one can do it that way as well, and the piecing together of the colours will appear incidentally. If you do the jigsaw puzzle properly you cannot but piece together the colours. The same I think is true of knowledge. If we are developing knowledge, if we are pursuing these objectives properly, then we are piecing together the development of the logical structures. But that does not mean that our timetable must be so constructed that we explicitly devote areas of time to doing this specifically. My analogy is of course very imperfect, because it does not bring out the fundamental nature of the conceptual structures and the tests for truth in knowledge. In the jigsaw puzzle the colours and the patterns on it seem to be at the same level and one could be pursued freely rather than the other. But that does not alter the point I want to make, that in fact one can design the curriculum in units which cut across divisions which are logically in the objectives, just as legitimately as one can design it to follow the logical organization.

There is then nothing in what I have said about the structure of objectives that *necessitates* curricular design in logically cohesive subjects. Nevertheless it does seem to me that there is here a presupposition that, if there are no reasons to the contrary, this is the most sensible way to organize the development of knowledge. It is then up to people to produce good grounds for structuring a curriculum in another way. Maybe, on motivational grounds, a curriculum should not be designed in terms of logically cohesive domains of knowledge. Maybe there are questions of mere convenience, of conditions in particular schools, or of particular people available, that mean the curriculum should be designed in some other way. If so, fair enough, but surely the case must be argued. What is important here is, I think, not to imagine that any one organization is *necessary* in this case, but to recognize rather that whatever programme one does produce, whatever structure one has for the curriculum, one is seeking to build up these logically cohesive areas of knowledge and to achieve other objectives dependent on such knowledge and understanding.

To be more specific, inter-disciplinary teaching on a topic basis is, I would suggest, a complex and highly difficult matter. If it is to be done rationally it must, for instance, be a topic in pursuit of which it is logically possible to achieve the objectives one wants. It seems to me highly irresponsible, educationally, to begin a topic if it is not explicitly designed to achieve predetermined objectives. And if a topic cannot achieve what one wants to achieve, then the topic should be discarded, not the objectives! But even if one has designed the topic as something that can be used to achieve set objectives, then what is demanded of teachers in terms of knowledge from different structures, teaching methods and collaboration with others, is tremendous. The demands of seriously, through-and-through, rationally planned curriculum work on a topic or project basis seem to me absolutely gargantuan. That is not to say that we should not try such work. But it can, I think, only be done in terms of the cooperation of the people who are aware of the different types of knowledge that are being contributed, who are expert in these, and who are determined to see that the objectives being sought in different areas are in fact achieved. It seems to me that only under these conditions can this form of learning be superior to the more traditionally subject-based approach. But I must add that curriculum units of any kind, be they subject or topic, are artificial units designed for the purposes of teaching. There is nothing primordial about traditional subjects. What we have to do is to look to that form of organization which is best suited to the circumstances, which will in fact achieve those objectives we are after. Undoubtedly we are nowadays looking for a new range of achievements both in the more traditional areas of knowledge and in newer areas of objectives that are coming into the curriculum. I see no reason why as a result the structure of the curriculum should not be fundamentally reconsidered.

I cannot close what I have to say without referring to one other problem – the structuring of the particular elements within a unit of the curriculum rather than within the curriculum as a whole. The precise significance of the work of Piaget in this area is a matter of dispute. Some have claimed, and I think with considerable force, that his stages in conceptual development may in fact be stages demanded logically by the nature of the concepts with which he is concerned. In that case, alternative stages of development are not logically possible, and no empirical investigation was necessary to find this out. A mere examination of how certain concepts presuppose others would have revealed the successive stages that Piaget refers to. That they occurred at certain ages is of course an empirical commentary on the particular circumstances associated with the children he in fact tested. If it is the case that the stages are simply logically necessary progressions in the development of concepts that children must go through if they are to understand later concepts, then this type of development is something which we can map out in areas of learning by philosophical analysis. The organization of content and methods in education can then be directly geared to the speeding up of these processes in so far as they are socially determined. It is the social and psychological conditions for learning that need to be empirically investigated, not the necessary stages of development. Certainly there is here a great area which needs to be investigated philosophically, logically and not just empirically. At last philosophers are beginning to get round to the job.[10]

Last of all, a comment about Bruner and the notion of the structure of knowledge which he uses in discussing the curriculum.[11] What he calls a structure is a quite specific organization of knowledge which he wishes to be pursued as an educational objective. He is concerned not with the range of necessary features of knowledge which I have referred to as forming a logical structure, for example, with orders of meaning of concepts that must be attended to if pupils are to understand at all. He is concerned with the fact that a knowledge of general principles, rather than of specific details, enables greater retention, makes knowledge more useful and is actually, from a learning point of view, altogether more economical. This is to pick out, from possible educational objectives in knowledge, certain quite specific ones and to suggest that to these should be given the principal attention of the curriculum. What he is doing then is not elucidating the logical structure of knowledge as a whole, pointing to necessary features, but saying that within the structure of knowledge as a whole there are certain objectives which we should consider most important of all. These he has shown empirically increase the quantity of knowledge learnt and the ability to use this knowledge. What therefore Bruner means by a structure of knowledge is a particular set of objectives which he considers important because of their general organizing character for other objectives. The big question then is whether Bruner is justified in stressing this limited range of objectives and by implication at least rejecting other lower level objectives in the learning of specific details. We must ask too about the emphasis on intellectual objectives and the neglect of other possible ends that seems to be involved. But these are not peculiarly philosophical questions.

I have tried to show at least some of the ways in which philosophy might contribute to rational curriculum planning. My account has been necessarily a kind of survey and one of work in many cases barely begun. I fear it has been abstract and very arid, but I hope I have communicated at least something of the fundamental importance of efforts in this area. Philosophy of education has indeed recently come to life in ways that mean that it can have no small influence for good on what goes on in the classroom. But for that to be the case there is a lot of hard analytical work to be done and at the moment there are too few people equipped to do the job. The opportunties for new curriculum developments in this country are growing and we are now awakening to the possibilities. The task is one that demands the collaboration of teachers and educationists of many kinds. It is bound to be difficult for these groups to understand one another's contributions, but I hope I have succeeded in making you just a little more aware than you were of the distinctive and important rôle philosophers have to play in this matter.

References

1 R. S. Peters, *Ethics and Education*, Allen and Unwin, 1966, ch. 1.
2 B. S. Bloom, *et al.*, *Taxonomy of Educational Objectives: Handbooks I and II*, Longmans Green, 1956, 1964.
3 For a fuller discussion of these issues, see R. F. Dearden, ' "Needs" in Education', *British Journal of Educational Studies*, November 1966.
4 See R. S. Peters, 'Emotions and the Category of Passivity', *Proceedings of the Aristotelian Society*, 1961-2.

M. Black, 'Rules and Routines', in R. S. Peters (editor), *The Concept of Education*, Routledge and Kegan Paul, 1967.

I. Scheffler, *Conditions of Knowledge*, Scott Foresman, Glenview, Illinois, 1965, ch. 5.

5 P. H. Phenix, *Realms of Meaning*, McGraw-Hill, New York, 1964, especially chs. 1, 2. Professor Phenix's work is clearly in the same philosophical tradition as the important work in the theory of knowledge by Ernst Cassirer, Suzanne Langer and Louis Arnaud Reid. All these have written much on different types of knowledge and experience that is important for curriculum planning. I have chosen to comment on Professor Phenix's work as he has written specifically in the context of curriculum development.

6 See P. H. Hirst, 'Liberal Education and the Nature of Knowledge', in *Philosophical Analysis and Education*, edited by R. D. Archambault, Routledge and Kegan Paul, 1965.

7 See the publications of The Farmington Trust, Oxford; director, John Wilson.

8 See I. Scheffler, *The Language of Education*, Thomas, Springfield, Illinois, 1960, chs. 4 and 5.

9 For discussion of some of the questions raised in this section, see R. S. Peters (editor), *The Concept of Education*, Routledge and Kegan Paul, 1967 (especially the papers by R. F. Dearden and J. P. White).

10 See D. W. Hamlyn, 'The Logical and Psychological Aspects of Learning', in R. S. Peters (editor), *The Concept of Education*, Routledge and Kegan Paul, 1967.

11 J. S. Bruner, *The Process of Education*, Harvard University Press: Oxford University Press, 1960.

The Contribution of History to the Study of the Curriculum

PAPER 3

Kenneth Charlton

THERE may be some among you who might ask, why should an historian be undertaking this subject? After all, the new star in the heavens which is called curriculum theory and development is very much concerned with the present and the future. Why call on an historian who is concerned with the past, a past which is dead and buried, or at the very least a past which cannot be known in the way the curriculum specialist knows about a curriculum?

And that may not be the only cause for doubt in your minds. Curriculum specialists nowadays talk in terms of models and theories, terms which historians rarely use. Some historians even deny them altogether. Again, curriculum theorists aim at generality and objectivity. Can history be general enough for curriculum theory? Can history be objective enough for curriculum theory? Paul Valery once described history as 'the most dangerous poison distilled in the crucible of the human mind', and Matthew Arnold regarded it as 'the vast Mississippi of falsehood'. Henry Ford, of course, regarded it as 'just bunk'. The possibilities of a contribution seem remote!

But, even if the past is not dead and buried, even if history is not subject to these particular disabilities, in what possible way can it contribute to thinking about such an up-to-date matter as curriculum theory and development? Before we can begin to answer such a question, however, the historian has to ask some questions of his own. To the curriculum theorist's question: 'Can history contribute to curriculum theory and development?', the historian might well reply: 'It depends, first of all, on what kind of theory you have in mind; and it depends, secondly, on what precisely it is you are theorizing about.' For unless the historian is clear as to what is meant by 'curriculum', and what kind of theory is considered appropriate for it, he would be hard pressed to know where to start. Herein, of course, lies the dilemma of meaning in intellectual discourse. If our terms are precisely defined they remain precise only if they are not widely used. If our terms are widely used they lose precision and produce confusion and misunderstanding rather than clarification, heat rather than light. And the problem is still further complicated when the plurality of knowledge (both in its content and in our means of achieving that content) is faced with the monolithicity implied in the term 'curriculum theory'.

As to the term 'theory', I take it that our curriculum specialist does not have in mind the man in the street's view which equates theory with idle armchair speculation, divorced from the evidence of the real world; nor that he wants to equate theory with 'doctrines' or 'philosophies'. Does he, then, insist that his curriculum theory is of the deductive-mathematical kind, a body of propositions consisting of postulates and theorems, where the postulates logically imply the theorems? Or is he happy to accept that such absolute logical rigour is inappropriate to his own study, and that theory is therefore to be thought of in terms of, say, a set of verified hypotheses, or of a conceptual framework which allows of and facilitates the systematic ordering of data. Has he in mind a structural model, or does he think of his theory as a set of prescriptive rules which lay down courses of action for given situations? Or does he prefer to accept B. O. Smith's enjoinder and consider his generalizing in terms of 'strategies'[1] rather than theories of a scientific kind with claims to the usual consistency, comprehensiveness and parsimony?

Curriculum theorists have not made up their minds about the precise nature of their theorizing. It would be surprising (and dangerous) if they had. I stress the differences, however, merely to emphasise the difficulty facing the historian who is asked to consider curriculum theory from his limited standpoint. For example, if the curriculum theorist wants to do his curriculum theorizing deductively, as George and Elizabeth Maccia have done,[2] then history's contribution might be of one particular kind. If, on the other hand, the theorizing is to be done inductively, history obviously will have to contribute in a different way. Certainly the latter method is nearer to the professional historian's approach, despite the fact that some historians would deny that they theorize at all. A. J. P. Taylor, for example, has insisted, 'I am not a philosophic historian; I have no system, no moral interpretation; I write to clear my mind, to discover how things happened and how men behaved.' We would do well, however, to remember Pascal's dictum that 'to reject philosophy is already to philosophize', and in the light of this to agree with Sir Keith Hancock that 'those historians who have no theory fill the vacuum with their prejudices'.[3]

As for the term curriculum, I take it that the curriculum specialist will want to think of it in extensive terms, and that his study (and therefore his theorizing) about it will take into account not only its content but also its methods, its objectives and even its evaluation. The question then becomes how can history contribute to decision making and theorizing about these aspects of the curriculum, or, to put it in more familiar terms, how can an historian contribute to the curriculum theorist's attempts to generalize about the why and the what and the how of the curriculum.

But before these questions can be answered we have also to ask ourselves, 'What is meant by history?' Or rather we have to ask the curriculum theorist to be clear what he means by history, and in what senses history is capable of offering a contribution. Does he have in mind that history can provide a deductive explanatory model? Or that history is an exercise of judgment? Does he think of history as a process of empathetic understanding? Or would he agree that history's model of narration is the model which most attracts him?

At one extreme end of a continuum history is thought of as

a deductive model borrowed from the physical sciences and at the other extreme end history is regarded as an unrelated series of unique events. In this kind of context then, we have to ask: 'Is history a different mode of experience from physical science, thus requiring a different method of investigation and explanation?', and we have to go on to ask: 'In what senses are classification, induction, experimental techniques, statistical quantification and so on appropriate research tools for the historian, as for the curriculum theorist?'

In the context of this paper, however, and to bring the problem down to reasonable proportions, history can be thought of in two senses: In the first place it can be thought of as 'the past', what we know about the past – something which can, perhaps, be used as data by the curriculum theorist, something which can provide the curriculum theorist with data from which he can learn 'lessons', and something even which might offer precise precedents on which to act in the future. Whatever use is made of history, however, in this sense we are concerned with the *content* of history.

In the second sense, on the other hand, history may be thought of as the historian's *method* or the historian's *discipline*. We are thinking here of his basic concepts and the methods of enquiry which he considers to be peculiarly appropriate to his trade. We then have to ask: 'How far are these concepts and methods likely to be of use in curriculum theorizing?'

Trying to answer the curriculum theorist's question, then, we can think of history as providing a model (of whatever kind), a model of procedure for curriculum building; or at the very least as contributing some small component of a model which might draw on several disciplines in its construction; or we can think of history as providing data from which a curriculum theory might be drawn, to explain which a curriculum theory might be formulated.

In a single paper one must perforce be selective, and perhaps arbitrarily so. I should like, therefore, to go on now to discuss (albeit all too briefly) four points which seem to me to be relevant to an historian's discussion of curriculum theory. I want to say something about models, about generality, about objectivity, and about tradition. First then, a word about models.

Curriculum theorists frequently discuss the use of models in their theorizing,[4] and yet the professional historian has traditionally been sceptical of this particular way of thought. H. A. L. Fisher, for example, reported that the more he sought a pattern in history, the less he was able to find one.[5] And those historians, or rather those writers, who claim to have found a pattern in history, are precisely the writers whom professional historians refuse to accept into the club. One has only to think of the reception of Arnold Toynbee's *Study of History*, or of those historians who seek to interpret Christian belief in their writing of history. The same kind of reception has been accorded to those writers who attempt to impose the model of evolution on the details of man's history. Palmerston, I imagine, was expressing a sentiment which many historians would echo sympathetically when he said, 'Half the wrong conclusions at which man arrives are reached by the abuse of metaphors, and mistaking general resemblance or imaginary similarity for real identity.'[6]

Yet, on the other hand, the historian makes use of a structural model the moment he assumes that the data he has assembled are ordered, or can be ordered and do not remain random. At the very least, he uses a narrative model, in accordance with which he arranges his data in chronological order, presumably on the assumption that this reflects a valid pattern and that at the same time it will enable him not merely to exhibit his data but also the better to offer an explanation of it.

Second, can history be general enough? The implication of this question is that curriculum theorizing can attain a level of generality similar to that of, say, the physical sciences, and assumes that the curriculum theorist is predominantly interested in universal laws or hypotheses which will enable him not simply to provide an explanation, at a high level of generality, of the data he collects, but also to predict from his formulated theory. Michael Oakeshott in his *Experience and its Modes* denies that the historian is concerned with generality at this level. The historian, he claims, is concerned with the description of particular events rather than the search for general laws which might govern these events: 'the moment historical facts are regarded as instances of general laws history is dismissed.'[7] To attempt to so regard them is to ignore a presupposition of historical enquiry, is to transform an historical way of investigating past events into a scientific one. For Oakeshott, the impossibility of explaining historical data on the scientific level is thus not simply an empirical one, a matter of mere practical difficulties. The difference is one of kind rather than of degree. And he is supported in his view by Sir Maurice Powicke who has proclaimed his adherence to 'a view of history which insists that some things happen because men and women with thoughts make them happen. Historical events are not like movements caused by the law of gravitation, they cannot be separated from what we call mind.'[8]

Even so, though the working historian does not as a rule search for general laws, he usually goes beyond Oakeshott's description of particular events. He goes beyond description to attempt also an explanation, and to do this he must go beyond the uniqueness of unique events in search of relationship between the events. As soon as he does this he raises the level of generality of his work, though without burning his fingers in the fire of prediction and prophecy.

Third, can history be objective enough? Once again the question implies a study objective enough for the curriculum theorist who wishes to take scientific objectivity as his model. The question is not (I take it) whether history is objective or not. Such a question is as unhelpful to the historian as it is to the scientist. Both would reply, 'It depends how high you set your standards of objectivity.'[9] My point here is not to set out a systematic argument to show that history may be thought of as sufficiently objective to enable it to contribute satisfactorily or appropriately to any consideration of curriculum theory. Here I can only assert that for the purpose of the curriculum theorist the content and discipline of history can be regarded as sufficiently objective to meet any requirements which he might insist upon.

It is true that, for Oakeshott, 'history is the historian's experience. It is made by nobody save the historian; to write history is the only way of making it', and in the same way Collingwood has insisted, with Croce, that 'all history is contemporary history'.[10] It is, of course, all too short a step from such a standpoint to the 'intrusion' of the historian and to the derogatory comments such as I mentioned at the beginning of this paper. But the study of history has gone a long way since the mid-nineteenth century when Positivism's influence on it was so strong. The relationship between knower and known is now recognized (by scientist and historian alike) to be much more complex than the Positivists supposed and insisted upon.[11]

In the same way, even though history does not share with science the search for general theories, it does demand the same kind of dedication, the same ruthlessness, the same passion for exactness as all the physical sciences. The historian binds himself by what is called his discipline, and in this sense he can claim an objectivity sufficient to persuade the curriculum theorist of his credentials, for I take it that neither the historian nor the curriculum theorist will claim for his study (or for the results of his study) an objectivity which will enable him to deduce conclusions from self-evident axioms.

Fourth, if we turn now from the method of history to its content we come right up against a concept in history which many theorists might well conclude would prevent history from contributing to curriculum theory. I refer here to the concept of tradition. For many a layman tradition has too easily been equated with the past, and has thus been considered to be a continual inhibiter of liberty, both of thought and of action, and therefore also of theorizing. Tradition, which imposes barriers on man's conduct and puts restrictions on his thought, is regarded as a despoiler of scrutiny, of disbelief, of scepticism, of receptiveness to the other point of view. Too often in the past we have seen the uncritical adulation of tradition, an adulation in which the past is always regarded as better than the present. It is this which has been the persistent enemy, it is claimed, of the liberal mind.[12] The dead hand of the past or the dead weight of tradition has suppressed individuality and selfhood. In this way, therefore, the past, equated with tradition, is regarded as being singularly unhelpful to an enterprise such as curriculum theory. On the other hand, the negative attitude to tradition which is expressed in a phrase such as 'the dead hand of the past', or 'the dead weight of tradition', reminds us that this absolute criticism of the past, as inevitably irrelevant and out-of-date, is equally destructive of practical decision-making. What is worse, both of these points of view are sustained by enthusiasms which themselves inhibit sceptical constructive scrutiny.

The concept of tradition is nevertheless one with which the curriculum theorist must concern himself, for he is already concerned with the curriculum of the past, either in a positive way, by doing some theorizing about it and perhaps bringing it up to date, or negatively by rejecting it altogether and building it anew. In one sense, however, the bedrock of the curriculum is that 'funded capital of social experience' which in some way must be handed on to a growing generation. Few curriculum theorists, I imagine, would deny this as part of the exercise, but we are concerned here not simply with the knowledge of the past, what might be called traditional knowledge, but also with the attitudes of the past. In an age of rapid change it may very well be that these have only a marginal impact on curriculum renewal, but in fact it would be virtually impossible to reject them totally. For example, we continue to think of curriculum in traditional terms if we think of it in terms of why, how, and what? These are questions which have been useful to ask in the past in guiding curriculum planning and they presumably will continue to be so.

The present problem of curriculum planning is itself shot through with the past and with vestiges of the past, and future solutions however radical will inevitably carry something of the past with them. Some of these vestiges are physical, in the form of existing textbooks, and more important, though perhaps less obvious because more subtle, in terms of school architecture, which may inhibit change and facilitate adherence to past procedures, methods and attitudes. (The same is recognized as a problem by penal reformers, who find that prison architecture of the late nineteenth century determines, to a much greater degree than they would wish, the procedures of dealing with present day prisoners.)

But the vestiges are not simply physical. More importantly they are vestiges of mental attitudes and values,[13] and once again we come up against the point of view which insists that the mental attitudes and the values of the past are better by definition than those of the present. This, I would have thought, is to go too far, but at the same time one has to beware of rejecting tradition absolutely, for though tradition reduces the rate of change in a society, in so far as it allows of a moderate rate of change it also enhances the orderliness of change. In the same way we can refer to the stability of tradition and the sustaining nature of tradition, both of which might be considered necessary if change is not to become anarchy. What is to be avoided is a position at extreme ends of the continuum. At one end are to be found the traditionalists for whom anything which once existed is entirely sacred by virtue of its very connectedness with the past, a sacredness which is untouchable and unchangeable and is endowed with an unquestioned inevitability. At the other end of the continuum are the rebels, who reject everything simply because it was once observed. Both of these positions are, of course, tarred with the same brush of ideology and extremism, and both are hostile not only to liberty but to tradition itself. 'The search for the usable past', as Edward Shils[14] has put it, is something which the curriculum theorist must be very much involved in.

The problem of tradition is, perhaps, even more crucial and even more complicated in curriculum theorizing in underdeveloped countries, where there is at one and the same time an even sharper wish to build anew (and to do so at a pace greatly exceeding that obtained by already developing nations) running alongside an even deeper pervasiveness of the past in both attitudes and practices, in which traditions are so hallowed as to be almost religious in character.[15] The situation is still further complicated by the fact that the society receiving (underdeveloped) and the society offering (developed) are differentially influenced by the past – in other words, have differential reactions to the past.

At all times, therefore, both the historian and the curriculum theorist have to remind themselves of the phenomenon of time-lag, or cultural time-lag, and this, too, is a matter of attitude as much as of practice. One has in mind here the lag between a set of values and social reality, a lag which was exemplified for example in the negative value judgments that were placed on usury at a time, in the fifteenth and sixteenth centuries, when interest paid on loans was an important and necessary feature of the expansion of credit. And we see it nearer at home in the continued use of the phrase 'scholarship class' in junior schools, and in references to a high percentage of pupils in a particular school 'getting through'.

If curriculum theorizing takes place in a simple traditional society, then the rôle of history is relatively easily identified. That which was preferred in the past provides the indubitable content, method and purpose and even method of evaluation. In other words, that content which has been used in the past, which has been transmitted by methods used in the past and for purposes which have been designated as acceptable in the past, provides the norm for future action. And if such content and method continue to produce the kind of person, the kind of citizen, which has been preferred in the past, then they will be deemed to be successful. The problem becomes rather more complicated, however, if history is expected to play a part in curriculum theorizing for a dynamic rather than a static society; though, referring back to our opening doubts, para- doxically for some people 'history' when invoked was con- sidered as antipathetic to change. The way in which the youth of today refer to fashions and indeed attitudes as 'ancient' is a good example of this.

Our model of curriculum theory must, then, include an element of time. It must include an awareness of the past, even if its purpose is to reject it, and an awareness of the future, even if only to recognize that some part of the past will remain to discolour its pristine newness. Furthermore, any curriculum which is devised as a result of the theorizing must include a component which helps sensitize a person first of all to his own past, and then to the past of others.

Our knowledge of the past should remind us, too, that though models with their various interconnected components are useful, they cease to remain so when the curriculum theorist imagines that component changes are uniform and regular, and happen at a predictable rate. In addition, we have to take into account not only the cultural time-lag to which I have referred, but we must also decide whether this is to be regarded as a good thing or a bad thing. Some people (and they need not be 'traditionalists') would regard this phenomenon as an expression of man's wisdom, or at least a useful safety valve (whether consciously devised by man or not), or even a defence mechanism. We must remember that the song, 'Fings ain't what they used to be', can evoke both hurrahs and boos. As Braithwaite reminds us, 'The price of the employment of models is eternal vigilance',[16] and in this case we have to make sure that the notion of change is both adequately represented and at the same time evaluated.

If the curriculum theorist thinks of his theory in tentative terms – that is, if he includes the factor of time in his model – he builds change into it, and his evidence for change is 'the past'. He thus builds a theory which is relevant to a particular kind of social situation, that is, not simply a situation which changes (for example, is expanding economically), but also one in which change is considered to be a good thing, for it is necessary in considering both of these points to remember that 'social change' as a concept is neutral, but that it can be accorded a positive or negative value. As a result a theory will be constructed that presumably will be able to cope with change in society in the future, a society which is not only changing itself but which is also likely to subject the theory to critical scrutiny, to modification and even rejection.

It is important to remember, also, that debates about the curriculum themselves have their roots in past attitudes and past value judgments, and an awareness of this should increase one's sensitivity to the debate. These attitudes can be positive, though possibly unconscious, in their carry-over of the past into the present. They can also be negative, in the sense that they represent a reaction against an irrelevant, dead-and-buried past. The basic premise of the debate is that the previous curriculum has been overtaken by the course of events, that it is out of date and therefore is in need of renewal. The task is different, then, from one in which the main problem is conceived of in terms of making more efficient the methods of the past.

Now these vestiges of the past are powerful because their influence is implicit, rarely explicit, unconscious rather than conscious. On the other hand, when tradition is called into account then the problem becomes conscious and explicit (though attitudes to the word tradition can, of course, be either positive or negative). History, then, can help us to put into context not only curriculum theory itself but our attitudes both to theory and to the activity of theorizing, and the complexity of these attitudes should remind us that we ignore at our peril those philosophical, political, social, economic, religious and other factors which a theoretician might well ignore in trying to base his curriculum renewal on purely educational grounds.

But context, and its multi-dimensional nature, is of importance, too, in so far as education is concerned to help the pupil understand his situation – that is, to understand himself in a context of others and of the natural world. What *I am*, however, and what my context *is*, comprehends not only the present. It comprehends also the past, the past of myself and of others, dead and alive, a past which may be thought of in terms of how I and my context have come to be what they are.

And at the same time it comprehends the future, what I hope to become and what I hope the context will become.

In linking the past with the present and the future, and in particular using the content of history, we have to beware of an amelioristic view of history which, for example, can say that 'the history of education might well be written in terms of the moving frontier of social conscience'.[17] This is uni-dimensional history which ignores the other forces at work in society, not simply those of politics, of religion, of economics and so on, but also those forces of indifference, apathy, ignorance and plain vested interest, all of which contribute to the shaping of institutions, attitudes and, of course, curricula. This is simply to say that the historian of education, say, is interested in the pathology of educational institutions, atti-tudes and curricula, as well as their ecology.

Even so, history can remind us that change is humanly possible, given the will and the opportunity for change. Without an awareness of the past we would be hard put to it to stand up and challenge arguments such as: 'It's not possible, human nature being what it is . . .' and so on. History reminds us not only that things do change (for good or ill, depending on one's value system), but also that things can be changed, that we can change them. The achievement of political equality in the past has been a good example of this, and as Professor Simon has reminded us, 'There is no more liberating influence than the knowledge that things have not always been as they are and need not remain so.'[18]

The history of curriculum renewal itself is a good guide on this score, given the assumption that we can and do learn from past experience, and that this is not to be considered the same as prophecy and prediction. To say this, however, is to say very little. We have to go on to ask in what way do we learn? To what degree do we learn? How much do we learn? We can see curriculum renewal at work in the education of the governing class in sixteenth century England, a renewal which took place despite the unwillingness of the traditional institu-tions of education to change their curricula to suit new demands.[19] In the same way we can compare the way in which the Comenians of the seventeenth century laid down a particular set of criteria for curricular planning, both in content and method, for the ordinary child, and we can see a different set of criteria at work in the reaction of the eighteenth century and nineteenth century Naturalists.

In fact, this kind of consideration has to be put in the context of a history of the nature of knowledge, or rather a history of man's view of knowledge. For example, what was termed natural philosophy in the mediaeval period included what we now call the physical sciences as well as the science of mind, and of course, philosophy itself. The increase in knowledge in the modern world has resulted from a division of labour which has produced the various subjects into which natural philosophy has been divided, and this has served its purpose. In the twentieth century, however, there appears to be a move towards a synthesis of knowledge, and this may very well lead us by the end of the century to a quite different approach to the nature of knowledge, and therefore of the curriculum and curriculum theory. In fact, this is already happening in our present day schools, in the formulation of actual curricula which aim at integrating the various components of the curriculum, and in so doing reflect new views about the nature of knowledge. It is important, too, to remember that every discipline has its own history, as has knowledge and our classification of it, our ways of achieving it, our ways of defining it. It would be a brave (or incompetent) man who would claim that his own discipline owes nothing to the past. His more perceptive colleagues will recognize that it still retains something of the past in its assumptions, implicit, unspoken and even unrecognized as these may be for some of his less perceptive colleagues.

I have tried, in this paper, to emphasise that any attempt by an historian to answer the question, 'How can history contribute to curriculum theory and development?' must first of all distinguish between the different views of history and the different views of curriculum theory which are current. Only then can he go on to deal with the substantive question, and this can be done in two ways. First of all he can consider the contribution which the structural disciplines of historical investigation, its concepts, its methods, can make, and secondly he can consider how far the content of history can be drawn on, not to provide particular and concrete answers or solutions to current problems, but to make us aware of the possibility of change, of the complexity of change, and of the carry over of the past into our present situation and future aspirations.

I can only hope that the points I have raised in this cautionary tale might be of help to those involved in theorizing about the curriculum of the past, present and future.

References

1   B. O. Smith, 'A Concept of Teaching', in B. O. Smith and R. H. Ennis (editors), *Language and Concepts in Education*, Rand McNally, Chicago, 1961, p. 100.
2   E. S. Maccia, *Methodological Considerations in Curriculum Theory Building*, presented to A.S.C.D. Commission on Curriculum Theory, Chicago, 1965.
3   A. J. P. Taylor, *Englishmen and Others*, Hamish Hamilton, 1956, p. 27.
    B. Pascal, *Pensées* i, 4.
    W. K. Hancock, 'Economic History at Oxford', in *Politics in Pitcairn and Other Essays*, Macmillan, 1947, p. 168.
4   Cf. E. S. Maccia and G. S. Maccia, 'The Ways of Educational Theorizing through Models', *Occasional Paper 62–111*, Educational Theory Center, Ohio State University.
5   H. A. L. Fisher, *A History of Europe*, Eyre and Spottiswoode, 1935, preface.
6   Cited E. Leach, 'Concepts: Models', *New Society*, 14 May 1964, p. 22.
7   M. Oakeshott, *Experience and Its Modes*, Cambridge University Press, 1933, p. 154.
8   F. M. Powicke, *History, Freedom and Religion*, Oxford University Press, 1938, p. 6.
9   Cf., for example, J. A. Passmore, 'The Objectivity of History', *Philosophy 33*, 1958, pp. 97–116; and C. Blake, 'Can History be Objective?', *Mind*, 64, 1955, pp. 61–78.
10 Oakeshott, op. cit., p. 99; and R. G. Collingwood, *The Idea of History*, Oxford University Press, 1946, pp. 282 ff.
11 Cf. Michael Polanyi, *Personal Knowledge*, Routledge and Kegan Paul,

1958, and *The Study of Man*, Routledge and Kegan Paul, 1959, especially Lecture III, 'Understanding History'.

12 Cf. E. Shils, 'Tradition and Liberty: antinomy and interdependence', *Ethics*, LXVIII (3), 1958, pp. 153–65.

13 K. Charlton, 'Tradition and Change in Sixteenth and Seventeenth Century English Education', *Year Book of Education*, Evans Bros., 1958, pp. 54–65.

14 E. Shils, loc. cit., p. 155.

15 Cf. A. Curle, 'Tradition, Development and Planning', *Sociological Review* (new series), VIII, 1960, pp. 223–38.

16 R. B. Braithwaite, *Scientific Explanation*, Cambridge University Press, 1953, p. 93.

17 H. L. Beales, *The Making of Social Policy*, Oxford University Press, 1946, pp. 21–2.

18 B. Simon, 'The History of Education', in J. W. Tibble (editor), *The Study of Education*, Routledge and Kegan Paul, 1966, p. 92.

19. Cf. K. Charlton, *Education in Renaissance England*, Routledge and Kegan Paul, 1965, part two.

The Contribution of Psychology to the Study of the Curriculum

Philip H. Taylor

IN any formal sense the study of the curriculum has hardly yet begun. By this I mean that the claims to know how it functions and under what conditions are not yet supported by an empirical and logical system of validation. Such a system has yet to be worked out. What I am here to ask is what psychology has to offer to those seeking to develop a curriculum theory and to improve curricular practices.

That the curriculum consists of content, teaching methods and purpose may in its rough and ready way be a sufficient definition with which to start. These three dimensions interacting are the *operational* curriculum. It is their interaction which gives rise to pupils' curricular experience and involves teachers in teaching. The outcome for pupils is intended to be attainments, achievements, skills, values, and beliefs.

Psychology, again to be very rough and ready, is about human behaviour under a variety of circumstances. That is, it is about describing it, explaining it, predicting it, and, of course, discovering more about it. Psychology is not, as is well known, a simple undifferentiated discipline. There are various branches or schools of psychology and within them there are specialisms each developing their own methods of procedure and their own technical language. In some respect each branch of psychology and each specialism may have something to offer to the study of the curriculum. But if it does, it will have to say something about the populations, the processes, or the products which are associated with the curriculum, or, of course, about the interactions of all three. The populations are the pupils and the teachers; the processes are the teaching methods which teachers use and the learning experiences which pupils undergo – or so we earnestly hope; the products are the abilities, the attainments, the skills, the attitudes, values and beliefs which are intended as the end points of pupils' curricular experience.

Psychology has certainly contributed a great deal to how children are regarded as pupils in schools and classrooms. No longer are they perceived as rather noisy buckets into which knowledge has to be pumped. The work of Susan Isaacs[1] and Valentine[2] has seen to this; so has the work of Bowlby and Piaget. They are perceived now as animate, self-aware, purposive, creative and developing, capable of feelings, thoughts and of establishing relationships. They may still be perceived by some to be at one or other stage of development but, as with the 'adolescence' of Stanley Hall,[3] such stages are fast fading to be replaced by a much more complex and dynamic picture.

Almost every aspect of the psychology of childhood has been and is continuing to be explored. The psychology of play, of moral development, of thinking is rigorously pursued, and each has had and is having its influence on the curriculum, on how pupils are perceived and treated by teachers, and how the content of the curricula is shaped by them to fit the pupil's state of readiness. In fact, the concept of readiness might not have become a familiar one in the language of teachers but for the influence of the psychology of child development. The best-selling *Curriculum Bulletin No. 1*, on primary school mathematics[4] is witness to the potent influence of Piaget; and the fact that both the 1931 Report on Primary Education[5] and the Plowden Report[6] contain sections of potted child psychology is witness to the official status it has achieved at least in respect of the primary school. The 1960 report on *Teaching Educational Psychology in Training Colleges*[7] showed that subjects such as child development, learning in children, and emotional development had then an important place in the education of teachers. The observation of particular children and the mapping of their behaviour is a common chore for students and an awareness of children's needs is stressed. In fact, the concept of needs has given rise in America, and to a lesser extent in this country, to a needs curriculum.[8] This had led to educational objectives being categorized in terms of the biological and psychological objectives of normal developments and the conditions which promote it. In turn this has led to the kind of statement of purpose for the curriculum which enshrines personal integration, self-fulfilment and experience. These terms have been derived by educationists from their study of the underlying assumptions implicit in the psychology of needs.

A great deal of child psychology is, however, descriptive, a-theoretic and uncluttered by rigorous empirical studies. There are few occasions in writing when conflicting and contradictory views of child psychology are explored and their nature made explicit. As a consequence many educators, for whom child psychology is a secondary study, hold a somewhat over-simplified view of the psychology of childhood, a view which fits in rather easily to a naturalistic or experience-orientated theory of education. In effect, a particular brand of child psychology is taken over as a model for education and out of this model particular ways of perceiving children and dealing with them emerges, and a curriculum is formulated. The 'free range' formula of the Plowden Report is a case in point. It is a formula (or a model) for the curriculum, at least of the primary school, which seems to find approval. The general concensus is that it works. But is this concensus sufficient criteria of validation?

Fortunately, it is not necessary for me to answer this question, though I will turn later to the general issue of which it is a part. It is perhaps sufficient for the moment for me to have indicated one way in which a particular branch of psychology has both contributed to the study of the curriculum and inhibited it at one and the same time – that is, by offering a model to educators which can readily be taken over and used. Let me hasten to add that I am not opposed to cross sorting[9] the application of the models of one field of study in the grounds of another. Much intellectual progress has come through doing this. All I am opposed to is to doing it naïvely without critical awareness.

But the models offered in the study of child psychology do not help all that much when we focus our attention on the processes of the curriculum, on learning experiences, for example: how they are created, what happens during them, and what they produce. Here we move into a field inhabited as much by animals as by humans – apes, cats, rats, pigeons and monkeys to name only a few – and into a field of technical language. Terms such as gestalt, stimulus, response, reinforcement, extinction, conditioning, and retroactive inhibition are legion. Both the animals and the terms have been pressed into service for the study of motivation, problem solving, thinking, remembering, attending, and understanding. Perhaps 'pressed into service' is far too mild a phrase for an area of study where there has been and is a great deal of rigour, where hypotheses are formulated, data amassed, and theories elaborated. In spite of all the work of Pavlov, Thorndike, Hull, Watson and Skinner and their students, remarkably little which is specifically identifiable seems to have found its way into the study of the curriculum. The general proposition that learning is a change in behaviour has become well rooted at least among transatlantic students of the curriculum. R. W. Tyler,[10] for example, has built his reputation on the proposition that the function of the curriculum is to bring about desirable changes in behaviour; that the purpose of the curriculum, at least at the tactical level, is to provide the kind of control which will direct a pupil's learning to worthwhile ends. The stress on the central learning function of the curriculum has directed many teachers' attention to the conditions for pupil learning, to the child rather than the subject matter. It has emphasized the conditions for promoting learning, but has left the 'what', the object of learning, rather suspended. When one reads what such students of the psychology of learning as Bugelshi[11] and Hilgard[12] have to say about the application of learning theory to education, one wonders whether they recognize the range and scope of the learning which teachers are expected to promote through the curricula they use.

Nevertheless, aspects of some of the general theories of learning have been taken over by teachers, studied and used in practice. The need for the active participation of the learner if learning is to take place has underpinned, if not given rise to, activity methods. The stress placed by teachers on the interest value of curricular materials has some relationship to what psychology has had to say about the motivation of learning, as has the stress which teachers now place on approval as a reward for learning. In fact, the whole area of reward and punishment in teaching has been influenced by the psychology of learning.

What has been missing until recently is interest in the business of learning for its own sake, something which is considered by many educationists to be a central feature, a basic characteristic of the curriculum. Psychologists are now studying concepts such as curiosity 'dressed up', as Peters[13] puts it, as 'the drive to know' or 'the exploratory drive'. In this work some students of the curriculum might find useful ways of looking at some curricular problems: at why, for example, some pupils become readily involved in curricular learning experiences and others do not.

The psychologists' study of needs and drives, of motives of one kind or another in the search for a theory of learning, have been extensive. Nor have they been confined to individual learning nor to the learning of narrow skills. They have reached out into group and social learning, into studies of thinking strategies and of the disposition to learn. They have embraced the rôle of language in learning and explored the problems of sequencing material for learning. From this some students of the curriculum have seen fit to concentrate their attention on the selection and organization of learning experiences which are seen by them as central issues in curriculum planning. Herrick[14] and Beauchamp[15] are cases in point. The work of Taba[16] and Bloom[17] show a similar bias –

a bias which, to put it precisely, concentrates attention on the learner, how he learns and why.

What now of the means of controlling this learning, of psychology's contribution to our understanding of teaching methods? There is a considerable literature on the psychology of training and instruction, as well as on such ancilliary trades as programmed learning and computer-assisted tuition which have grown up around it. But training is one thing, teaching another and bigger thing altogether, though a psychologist like Skinner[18] would not have us believe so. That training and instruction have a part to play in teaching would be hard to dispute and it is naturally to be expected that some teachers see in the psychology of training much of relevance to them in curricular matters. In fact, the work of Glaser,[19] Lumsdaine,[20] and Gagné,[21] as well as that of their forerunners Skinner and Crowder, has had some influence on thinking about the curriculum. For one thing, it has drawn attention to the value of analysing the task to be presented to pupils in order to present it more effectively, to the value of such instructional devices as auditory and pictorial aids to instruction and to the development of a range of self-instructional techniques. However, with such attractive exceptions as Thornhill's programmed texts, particularly his *The Waterloo Campaign*, the influence of this work on teaching methods has not been so far significant.

On the other hand, some work by psychologists on teaching methods may have had a considerable reinforcing influence. The work of Kersh[22] on learning by discovery is a case in point. Almost every curriculum development project today stresses the discovery method, a stress which is acceptable to almost all teachers. It is already a part of their stock in trade, taken on as an approved pedagogical procedure. But psychology may have done no more than provide marginal support for it as a teaching method from the studies which have been conducted.

Some psychologists are sceptical of these studies. Cronbach,[23] for example, doubts whether they have been conducted in conditions which can be claimed to be anything like the conditions of the classroom in which they are employed, or over the kind of time scale which is of relevance to teaching. Certainly most of the studies have been confined to a very limited range of subject matter.

But students of the curriculum seek from psychology guidance on teaching methods and, when they do not get it from relevant studies, tend to 'manufacture' it for themselves. A classic case is Herbert Read's *Education through Art*[24] where the work of the gestalt school of psychology was pressed into service to underpin the child-centred curriculum which was at its heart. None of the 'manufactured' teaching methods so derived have been verified by empirical study. They have been taken on the nod, as it were.

Turning to the products of the curriculum, to the desirable changes in behaviour which the curriculum is designed to cultivate; to the skills, abilities, attainments, attitudes, values and the beliefs which teachers desire to develop through the matter and methods which they employ – this is an area on which much attention has been focused. For the teacher working with curricular materials it represents what they are striving after, at least in the short run. For the psychologist it represents, in many cases, the operational criteria against which to verify their hypotheses. The study of skills and abilities and the differences in them between individuals has occupied a respected place in psychology since psychology broke away from philosophy some time in the nineteenth century. The most noteworthy (or, as some educationists would say, notorious) of these skills and abilities is, at least in the context of the study of the curriculum, 'intelligence'. The disputes about what it is, what factors support its nurture and where it belongs in the iconstellation of cognitive skills have produced a very considerable literature. But the more important literature by far is that concerned with attempts to develop theories about the location of intelligence in the structure of the mind. From the early work of Spearman[25] to the recent work of Hebb,[26] psychologists have attempted to account for 'intelligence' and how it operates. And these attempts have influenced our thinking about the curriculum, not only about the suitability of its content for particular groups of pupils, but also about the extent to which a curriculum can contribute to the nurture of intelligence. Thus, we find in the Minister's Foreword to the Newsom Report[27] the statement 'that all children should have an equal opportunity of acquiring intelligence . . .'

The work of Husen,[28] Lovell[29] and others supports this assertion, as does the theoretical work of Hebb. But is the term 'intelligence' used in the same way by both psychologists and educators? About this issue we should, to put it midly, have doubts and reservations. Nevertheless, in thinking about curricular content and in the planning of curricula the psychology of intelligence has had considerable influence. And it would be to everyone's disadvantage, psychologists and educationists alike, to assert that this influence was only to be regretted. What is needed is a careful critical appraisal of the nature of this influence, so that both psychologists and educationists learn to apply psychological constructs to educational problems more cautiously in the future. Most psychological constructs partake of the characteristics of models or 'as if' pictures and it is important to be very much aware of this, and not to mistake the models for the things which they model. As philosophers of science such as Braithwaite[30] say, 'The price of the employment of models is eternal vigilance,' in this case, vigilance about the model implied in the construct intelligence. Hofstaetter and Ferguson's papers in a recent collection of readings on intelligence and ability[31] should be read with this salutory exercise in mind. Hofstaetter shows how the meaning to be attributed to the term intelligence, as operationally defined in tests of intelligence, varies with the age group being tested, and Ferguson shows (as does Cattell[32] in his discussion of crystallized and general intelligence) that the construct intelligence has both a specific, workaday reference and a long-term cultural meaning.

What I have said about intelligence applies also to other constructs commonly to be found in education and psychology.

Achievement and aptitude are two such constructs. Their operational definition is frequently both woolly and unstable. Over even short periods of time, it is difficult to be confident that there have not been basic shifts in emphasis.

Of course, this need not be so. Psychologists since Galton have been busily developing the field of psychometrics with the aid of sophisticated technical expertise. Both psychological and educational measurement call on it and it can provide both stable and precise assessments of curricular products, given, of course, that we are willing and able to accept the operational definitions as models of the reality they seek to assess. And there is no shortage of enterprise in this field as anyone who cares to consult the *Mental Measurement Yearbook*[33] can see for himself.

Constructs such as intelligence, ability and aptitude have tended to be used both as a guide to the level of curricula for groups of pupils and as a means of assessing the pay-off in particular curricular experiences. Any set of constructs used of this double way is at risk. Mainly, the risk is of self-deception, of believing that one has proved the case when in fact the judge, jury and witnesses are one and the same. This is a kind of psychological Zen Buddhism taken to absurdity, and accounts for why the many so-called method experiments in educational psychology come up with results which are at variance with observed reality. Douglas's *Home and School*[34] study is a classic instance. None of his 'within school' findings is worth much. And, if the study of the operational curriculum is to make progress, it must take care to avoid the risks involved in using constructs in a double way to measure both the input and output. It is to the psychometrics of change in performance that it must look for guidance – and pretty complex guidance it will be, too.

Aptitudes and abilities are one thing, attitudes, values and beliefs another. But they represent a domain of objectives which, equally with skills and abilities, the curriculum is concerned to cultivate. It is from the psychology of personality development and structure that contributions to this aspect of

the study of the curriculum have come: from Freud and
Cattell, from Lewin and Allport, and from Murphy and
Eysenck. Not only have psychologists studied personality, both
in itself and in its social context, they have also studied character. In doing so they have used technical constructs: the ego,
the id, the super-ego, the self-concept, anxiety, guilt-proneness,
and, of course, the surgency, character strength, parmia, and
ergic tension of Cattell.

A great deal of this work in the psychology of personality
has armed students of the curriculum with both the means for
measuring its product – the changes in behaviour which it
produces – and the terms for describing and defining it
operationally. *Handbook 2* of Bloom's *Taxonomy of Educational
Objectives*[35] is an indication of the range of this influence: from
'awareness' to 'characterization' through 'willingness to
respond' to 'commitment'.

Some of the studies undertaken under the influence of the
psychology of personality have been depressing. They have
suggested that the curriculum of schools and colleges stamps
in conforming behaviour and irrational-conscientious character
traits as well as inhibiting the growth of altruistic impulses.[36]
They have also indicated the over-simplified view which
many teachers have of the personalities and values of their
pupils.[37]

In fact, both the psychology of abilities, general and specific,
and the psychology of personality have offered a methodology
of what has been called 'curriculum accountancy'. What price
desirable changes in behaviour? What profit and loss to the
individual and to the community?

To return to a population variable, what of the teacher? It is
in his behaviour that the curriculum comes to life. He sets the
tasks and creates the conditions for their achievement. What
has psychology got to offer? Has it helped in the study of
teacher effectiveness? Certainly the psychology of interpersonal relationships, of leadership and of social interactions
has stimulated a whole range of studies which are important
if we are to understand the processes of the curriculum of

which the teacher is frequently the instigator, mediator and, as often as not, the judge of its effectiveness.

The classic work of Lippit and White[38] on the relationship between leadership rôles and the social climates of youth clubs started an exploration into the structure of instructional groups of all kinds which is still vigorously under way some thirty years later. Lewin and his co-workers, using a theory of social psychology which drew heavily on gestalt theory and on an adaption of mathematical vector theory, tried to show that different styles of leadership – authoritarian, democratic and *laissez faire* – promoted different kinds of behaviour in the boys in the group, and how experience of different styles of leadership impinged on attitudes to and readiness to accept other and opposed styles of leadership.

This work led to the studies of Anderson and Brewer[39] on the dominative and integrative behaviour of classroom teachers, and more recently to Flanders's work on direct and indirect teacher behaviour.[40] Lewin's theory of social psychology has been replaced by the interaction process-analysis theory of Bayles[41] in which, to put it crudely, two areas within any group, instructional or otherwise, are identified as the source of behaviour – a task area, and a socio-emotional area. Within groups individuals can relate to one or the other – that is, they can perceive them as the relevant areas as far as they are concerned. And it is to these areas that the transactions of teachers with pupils and pupils with teachers can be construed to have relevance. Thus Flanders, in studying the verbal behaviour of teachers, sees their verbal acts as having this kind of relevance to the task or to the supportive (or destructive) area of interpersonal relationships and feelings. Teachers who carry the task on the shoulders of interpersonal relationships, Flanders calls 'indirect'. Teachers who do not, he calls 'direct'. By using such a backing to studies of the classroom, Flanders can state 'that student achievement and attitude scores were significantly higher for those classes in which the teachers were more indirect'. And when Flanders's work is pushed further it becomes possible to state: 'Indirectness (of the teacher) seems to be negatively associated with the development of children who are distractible and show attention-getting insecurity'.[42]

In short, the picture which is emerging from the application of psychology to the classroom process accords with that of the trained observer who perceives, for instance, that the teacher who works outward from the children has no difficulty in controlling the behaviour of children who have a low tolerance of a restrictive environment. But it would be wrong to suppose that the purpose of psychological studies of the classroom is to win the approval of trained observers, no matter who they are or how well trained. And equally wrong to suppose that such findings must (or need) accord with common sense, whatever that is.

The purpose and value of such studies as these must in the end be related to the extent to which they contribute to a general theory of the classroom process. Such a theory is most likely to arise where the findings of one research are used as the hypotheses of the next, and where the constructs which underpin the research are made explicit. The outcome of such activity might well be a language both for talking about the processes of the curriculum, including teaching, which is unambiguous, and for making prediction of causal connections more certain.

But there are likely to be many false leads in the search for such predictions. Already the study of the emotional climates of instructional groups, of leadership in the classroom and of the interpersonal relationships between pupil and pupil have led into blind alleys – at least so far as education is concerned. However, there is hope that the work of such people as Flanders, Bellack[43] and Gump[44] will lead to something like solid ground because it is concerning itself with desirable (or should I say desired) curricular outcomes. Such work has made the progress which it has on the back of a theory of social psychology. This educationists should not forget.

Teaching is at the centre of the operational curriculum. Teachers may not be. The psychology of teachers as such may be of interest to psychologists and even to teachers but not, I would suggest, to students of the curriculum. Perhaps the most disappointing application of psychology to teaching was Ryan's study of teacher characteristics.[45] What came out of it was that teachers are about as much like the general run of adults as could be. It is *the teacher in the act of teaching*, as the manager of a purposeful environment aiming to promote the intrinsic appreciation of worthwhile activities, which should be the objective of attention. Psychology provides a range of tools for this study, tools both conceptual and methodological.

In what is, at least to my knowledge, the most complete study of a curriculum in operation yet undertaken, psychology has been used for three purposes:

1. as a guide to the structuring of the subject matter for learning and teaching;
2. as a source of empirical methodologies for studying how the curricular materials are transacted in teaching;
3. similarly, as a source of methodologies, of instrumentation for the evaluation of outcomes.[46]

Gestalt theory was used because it seemed to the curriculum developers the model which best facilitated the development of curricular materials. With all the data on teaching and learning to hand, it should be possible to assess whether or not it was an adequate model. I do not know whether this is being undertaken or not, but it strikes me that this may be one important way of using psychology in studying the curriculum.

It is on this note of using psychology that I would like to move toward a conclusion. I mentioned earlier in my comments on the influence of the psychology of child development how psychology was used to justify curricular decisions and practices, and I noted, at least by implication, how a psychological concept such as that of *needs* can be displaced to validate curriculum planning. I suggested also that a certain amount of 'manufacturing' of psychology went on to assist in providing a gloss of scientific respectability to curricular proposals. None of these ways of using psychology seems to me to be legitimate, and educationists have themselves to blame if any of these ways of using psychology turns out to inhibit the progress of our understanding of education, and of the way in which the curriculum functions. The only valid way of using psychology is in full awareness of its nature, of whether it is still relatively unverified theory one is using or whether it is more than a construct or term. Theories and constructs from psychology will prove useful and valid in studying the curriculum only in so far as we can remember that they are on loan and that they belong to psychology, not to education.

Certainly, and as is plain, psychology can provide students of the curriculum with models for perceiving their observations and methods for organizing their data, but it cannot account for all that is associated with curriculum, for many of the choices which are made, or for the desirability or otherwise of the outcomes. And it would be better if more of those who try to study the curriculum tried harder to apply their psychology as rigorously as do psychologists – or as most of them do. For not all psychologists are rigorous. Some, like Bruner,[47] have a liking for the grand design. They stimulate, certainly, and, almost as easily, convince the unwary. For psychologists, such men may be providing the theories of tomorrow. Educationists cannot wait so long. Theirs is to do what they can to use the psychology of today to improve the educational practices of today. They are also under obligation to use what is on loan to them from psychology within the terms of that loan and to prevent its abuse. By doing only the latter, our understanding of the operational curriculum would become more certain. To do the former, and so be more aware of the nature of the psychology we use as a model *for* (and not *of*) certain aspects of the curriculum, might bring us the confidence that we can make tractable such curricular problems as the prediction of the effects of a teacher's behaviour. And I have no need to stress how high is such a reward.

However, there is a final condition to be met if there are to be rewards. Statements about the curriculum must be made in terms which are susceptible of disproof by empirical means if psychology is to be of help in the development of a formal theory of the curriculum. Psychology is a science and as such is governed by a morality or code of rules which calls for the empirical verification of its propositions. Its purpose is to elaborate an increasingly comprehensive theory of human behaviour. The curriculum is something other than this. It is not a subject, but rather a set of practical activities and the purpose of its study is to improve the efficiency of the practical activities associated with it. Psychology, as I hope I have shown, can help us grasp the nature of these practical activities more effectively and by so doing improve one area of education. But it will only do this if educationists are very clear about the rôle of psychology and aware that its goals and those of the curriculum are different.

References

1 S. Isaacs, *The Children we Teach*, University of London Press, 1932.
2 C. W. Valentine, *Psychology and its Bearing on Education*, Methuen, 1950.
3 G. S. Hall, *Adolescence*, Appleton, New York, 1905.
4 Schools Council, *Curriculum Bulletin, No. 1: Mathematics in the Primary School*, H.M.S.O., 1965.
5 *The Primary School*, H.M.S.O., 1931.
6 Central Advisory Council, *Children and their Primary Schools*, H.M.S.O., 1967.
7 British Psychological Society, *Teaching Educational Psychology in Training Colleges*, British Psychological Society, 1962.
8 J. G. Saylor and W. M. Alexander, *Curriculum Planning for Modern Schools*, Holt, Rinehart and Winston, New York and London, 1966.
9 C. R. Turbayne, *The Myth of Metaphor*, Yale University Press, 1962.
10 R. W. Tyler, *Basic Principles of Curriculum and Instruction*, University of Chicago Press, 1950.
11 B. R. Bugelski, *The Psychology of Learning Applied to Teaching*, Bobbs-Merrill, New York, 1956.
12 E. R. Hilgard, *Theories of Learning*, Appleton Century, New York, 1956.
13 R. S. Peters, *Ethics and Education*, Allen and Unwin, 1966.
14 J. B. MacDonald, D. W. Anderson, and F. B. May, *Strategies of Curriculum Development* (Selected Writings of Virgil E. Herrick), Charles Merrill Books, Columbus, Ohio, 1965.
15 G. A. Beauchamp, *Curriculum Theory*, Kegg Press, Wilmette, Illinois, 1961.

16 H. Taba, *Curriculum Development*, Harcourt Brace and World, New York, 1962.

17 B. S. Bloom, *et al.*, *Taxonomy of Educational Objectives: Handbook I, The Cognitive Domain*, Longmans Green, 1956.

18 B. F. Skinner, 'The Science of Learning and the Act of Teaching', in A. A. Lumsdaine and R. Glaser (editors), *Teaching Machines and Programmed Learning*, National Educational Association of the U.S. (N.E.A.), Washington, D.C., 1960.

19 R. Glaser (editor), *Teaching Machines and Programmed Learning*, vol. II, *Data and Directions*, N.E.A., Washington, D.C., 1965.

20 A. A. Lumsdaine and R. Glaser (editors), *Teaching Machines and Programmed Learning*, N.E.A., Washington, D.C., 1960.

21 R. M. Gagné, *et al.*, 'Factors in Acquiring Knowledge of a Mathematical Task', *Psychological Monographs*, 76, 1962.

22 B. Y. Kersh, 'The Motivating Effect of Learning by Directed Discovery', *Journal of Educational Psychology*, vol. 53, 1962, p. 66.

23 L. J. Cronbach, *Experiments in Discovery*, 1962 (personal paper).

24 H. Read, *Education Through Art*, Faber and Faber, 1943.

25 C. Spearman, *The Abilities of Man*, University of London Press, 1927.

26 D. O. Hebb, *The Organisation of Behaviour*, John Wiley, New York, 1949.

27 Central Advisory Council, *Half our Future*, H.M.S.O., 1963.

28 T. Husen, 'The Influence of Schooling on IQ', *Theoria*, 17, 1951.

29 K. Lovell, 'Intellectual Deterioration in Adolescents and Young Adults', *British Journal of Psychology*, 46, 1955, pp. 199–210.

30 R. B. Braithwaite, *Scientific Explanation*, Cambridge University Press, 1953; Harper and Row, New York, 1960.

31 S. Wiseman (editor), *Intelligence and Ability*, Penguin, 1966.

32 R. B. Cattell, *The Scientific Analysis of Personality*, Penguin, 1965.

33 O. K. Buros, *Mental Measurement Yearbook*, Gryphon, 1964.

34 J. W. B. Douglas, *Home and School*, MacGibbon and Kee, 1964.

35 D. Krathwohl, *et al.*, *Taxonomy of Educational Objectives: Handbook II, The Affective Domain*, Longmans Green, 1964.

36 D. Havighurst and C. Peck, *The Psychology of Character Development*, Appleton Century, New York, 1960.

37 H. J. Hallworth, 'Anxiety in Secondary Modern and Grammar School Children', *British Journal of Educational Psychology*, vol. 43, 1961, p. 55.

38 R. Lippit and R. K. White, 'The Social Climate of Children's Groups', in R. G. Barber, J. S. Kounin, and H. F. Wright (editors), *Child Behaviour and Development*, McGraw-Hill, New York, 1943.

39 H. H. Anderson and J. E. Brewer, 'Studies of Teachers' Classroom Personalities', *Applied Psychological Monographs*, Nos. 6 and 8, 1945 and 1946.

40 N. A. Flanders, 'Teacher Influence, Pupil Attitudes and Achievement', *Co-operative Research Monograph*, No. 12, U.S. Department of Health Education and Welfare, 1965.

41 R. F. Bales, *Interaction Process Analysis*, Addison-Wesley, Reading, Massachusetts, 1950.

42 T. A. Birkin and P. H. Taylor, 'Notes toward an Instructional Theory', paper read at the Invitational Seminar: *Next Steps in Research into Teaching*, O.I.S.E., Toronto, 1967.

43 A. A. Bellack, J. R. Davity, *et al.*, 'The Language of the Classroom', Co-operative Research Project No. 1497, U.S. Department of Health Education and Welfare, 1963.

44 P. V. Gump, 'Setting Variables and Projection of Teacher Behaviour', *Proceedings of the Annual Meeting of the American Educational Research Association*, 1967.

45 D. G. Ryans, *Characteristics of Teachers*, American Council on Education, Washington, D.C., 1960.

46 M. Lovenstein, E. J. Furst, *et al.*, *Development of Economics Curricular Materials*, Co-operative Research Project, Research Foundation, Ohio State University, 1966.

47 J. S. Bruner, *The Process of Education*, Harvard University Press: Oxford University Press, 1960.

PAPER 5

The Contribution of Sociology
to the Study of the Curriculum

Frank Musgrove

In his introductory paper, Professor Kerr distinguished between four interrelated components of the curriculum – curriculum objectives, knowledge, learning experiences, and curriculum evaluation. So far, sociology has contributed principally to the determination of objectives. I believe that sociology has been misapplied in this connection, although sociological investigation can properly provide evidence to help philosophers and policy-makers reach their decisions. Sociological inquiry is long overdue in the field of evaluation, but this task is extremely difficult. The curriculum often has social objectives, and we have very little evidence that these are attained. But I believe that the important contribution of sociology to curriculum studies is neither in the field of objectives nor of evaluation; more modestly, I would claim that sociology can promote an understanding of the curriculum as a social system. By examining the functioning (and malfunctioning) of the curriculum in these terms, the sociologist may help us to understand certain obstacles to change, and make us aware that curriculum development is in part a social problem calling for social solutions.

It is curious that sociology has been used mainly for deciding what the content of the school curriculum ought to be. Notably in the writings of the late Sir Fred Clarke, sociology has been invoked to arrive at judgments about curriculum objectives. I do not say that this is an entirely illegitimate exercise, but we need to be clear about the sort of questions sociology can, and cannot, answer. Sociologists who have interested themselves in the school curriculum have not always appreciated the limitations of their discipline.

Since the time of Durkheim sociologists have been interested in social, as distinct from psychological, facts. 'Social facts' were a central preoccupation of Fred Clarke. In his educational writings in the nineteen-thirties and forties, and in his capacity as chairman of the Central Advisory Council for Education after the war, Clarke has deeply imprinted his own interpretation of a 'social fact' on our thinking about the curriculum.

Social facts were seen by Durkheim as incapable of explanation in terms of individual psychology, if only because they exist outside and apart from individual minds. A language, for example, is there before an individual is born into the society which speaks it, and it will be there after he is dead. He merely learns to speak it, as his forefathers did and as his descendants will. It is a social fact which can only be understood in relation to other facts of the same order. The individual merely passes through the social structure. It was not born with him and does not die with him. The totality of social facts which compose the social structure are external to the individual and obligatory.

I think a lively awareness of the nature of social facts is important when we are thinking of the content and purpose of a school curriculum. It is a sobering and even dispiriting concept for educationists, suggesting limits to what can be achieved by influencing individual minds. It provides a valuable corrective to the utopian planning to which curriculum reformers are prone. Many curricular changes have been introduced in recent decades in an attempt to modify undesirable social facts – rates of marital breakdown, death on the roads, racial segregation, international strife. I do not say that education can make no contribution to these problems, but racial conflict, the incidence of divorce and rates of death on our roads are all social facts; they will be changed when we alter other social facts which bear upon them, and not simply by modifying our school curricula. The obstinate level of road deaths in spite of determined road safety campaigns perhaps best illustrates my point. We can teach road safety, but we shall not make any significant change in the rate of road deaths at Christmas until we change our institutionalized holiday arrangements and our conventions of conviviality. We need a more thorough understanding of social causation if we are to use our educational institutions efficiently, economically and appropriately. (The evaluation of the curriculum in terms of its social objectives is a problem I will return to later in this paper.)

The trouble with Fred Clarke was that he invested social facts with a moral significance. It is one thing to recognize their stubborn externality; it is another to claim that because they exist they have a moral right to be perpetuated. But the alleged moral obligation of social facts has been a powerful reason for reflecting the local world in the school curriculum and adapting our subjects to the immediate environment.

In the writings of Fred Clarke, 'culture' as understood by anthropologists (or at least by Ruth Benedict), 'social facts' as understood by Durkheim, and 'the General Will' as understood by Rousseau are all equated or combined into an overriding social imperative. But cultures, subcultures and social facts are merely conceptual tools for examining what *is*; the philosophical concept of the General Will tells us what ought to be. It told Fred Clarke that, 'It is the first business of education to induce conformity in terms of the culture in which the child will grow up', that the overmastering purpose of education is 'the production of the given citizen type'.[1]

These ideas are developed in their most sophisticated form in *Freedom in the Educative Society*, published in 1948. Their seeds are to be found in *The Year Book of Education* for 1936 to which Clarke contributed a chapter on 'The Conflict of Philosophies'. Here he is already announcing that: 'Whatever else education may mean, it must mean primarily the self-perpetuation of an accepted culture – a culture which is the life of a determinate society.' And social facts appear, too, in almost straight (if unacknowledged) translation from Durkheim: 'It is the authority of the society to which the English child belongs', maintains Clarke, 'that requires him to call a certain animal *dog* rather than *chien* or *hund*. So, too, with the forms of grammar, the technique of writing, and a thousand other skills and attainments that go to the forming of his achieved personality. That a thing is this way rather than that, that you speak this rather than some other way: these things come in the first instance on social authority. They are not really matters within the child's choice unless his education is to go all awry.'

But it is not the sociologist, Durkheim, but the philosopher, Rousseau, who is invoked by Clarke to provide moral authority for social conformity. Rousseau's General Will is also external to the individual and it is certainly morally obligatory; to induce obedience to it is to force a man to be free. Fred Clarke is all for forcing children to be free. 'The true sanction of authority for the child', he says, 'is that he should be able, sooner or later, to recognize in it himself, his own will as it would be, were he more fully enlightened. The justification is the same as that which Rousseau adduces of obedience to the General Will.'

All this may seem far removed from the practicalities of curriculum construction. But at the level of educational policy making we find Clarke's influence dominating such important publications as *School and Life* which appeared in 1947, and *The Curriculum and the Community in Wales*, which was published in 1952. In curriculum design the local subculture assumes an awful significance. *School and Life* is peppered with such pronouncements as: 'A school is always, wherever and whatever it is, part of a social unit; and it cannot escape the consequences of its geographical situation' and 'different environments should be taken into account in planning the curriculum of the schools which are in them . . . the curriculum should be so designed as to interpret the environment to the boys and girls who are growing up in it.'

There may be good reasons for devising our curricula in the light of the local environment; all I am questioning is the kind of sociological argument that brought Fred Clarke to this view. And the view is stated in more extreme form in *The*

Curriculum and the Community in Wales. Here the sociological substructure shows through more obviously. The curriculum in Wales should rest firmly on the culture of Wales, for 'all education implies community and some degree of conformity. If the needs of the child are rightly understood, we must insist that any view of personality is defective which does not see the individual as a member of a community and that therefore education will only be truly child-centred when it recognizes that it must in some sort conform to something that is "external" to the child, namely a pattern of life and ideals cherished by the community, in other words to a culture.' 'For our concern,' continues the report, 'is not to describe the Welsh way of life, but to preserve it.'

Such sociological arguments have a more sinister ring when they are used – as they are – to justify the social and educational policy of apartheid in South Africa. It is true that Fred Clarke attempted, with delightful inconsistency, to make provision for 'growth beyond the type'. But in any case sociology is being used to do a job which it cannot do. My complaint is about the *abuse* of sociology in relation to thinking about the curriculum. The jobs which it can properly do have scarcely been attempted.

Sociology, as I have said, is concerned with the facts of organized human relationships. It will illuminate our understanding of the curriculum by revealing school subjects not simply as intellectual, but as social, systems. I do not say that sociology thus conceived will make a directly practical contribution to detailed curriculum design, but it will deepen our understanding of the activity in which we are engaged.

And as a deliberate and systematic organization of experiences and relationships, I think we see the curriculum first and foremost as an artificial device, a contrivance, in some sense an unnatural arrangement. It is properly artificial, selecting, organizing, elaborating and speeding up many of the processes of real life.[2] I think that when we see the curriculum in these terms, we see it for the important mechanism that it is; we are less inclined to rely on a sort of pseudo-schooling which has abdicated in favour of apparently lifelike arrangements and importations. It is all much more difficult, and requires more deliberate effort, than simply exposing children to lifelike situations.

The business of the sociologist is to explore the systematic social relationships on which this artificial contrivance depends. He will examine subjects both within the school and in the nation at large as social systems sustained by communication networks, material endowments and ideologies. Within a school and within the wider society subjects are communities of people, competing and collaborating with one another, defining and defending their boundaries, demanding allegiance from their members and conferring a sense of identity upon them. They are bureaucracies, hierarchically organized, determining conditions of senior membership, establishing criteria for recruitment to different levels, disciplining their members through marks of recognition like honorary fellowships and admission to exclusive inner councils. Even innovation which appears to be essentially intellectual in character can be usefully examined as the outcome of social interaction and the elaboration of new rôles within the organization.

Studies of subjects in these terms have scarcely begun, at least at the school level. De Solla Price and Hagstrom in America[3] and Ben-David in Israel[4] have examined the organization and growth of scientific subjects in their higher reaches in this way, but such a sociology of the school curriculum is not yet in sight.

Curriculum development is not simply a question of presenting new kinds of knowledge, new combinations of knowledge and providing new kinds of learning experience; it involves teachers (and pupils) in new social rôles. Many of the setbacks to curriculum development since the Second World War are to be attributed less to the intrinsic character of new methods and content than to the difficulties of making new social rôles acceptable. To ask a physics graduate to take general science or an historian to take social studies is not only to expose him as a narrow specialist, it is to threaten his sense of identity.

We need to recognize – and still more, we need to investi-
gate – the function of subjects, particularly at their more
advanced levels, in conferring a sense of identity. In middle
and late adolescence, identification with a school subject must
increasingly take the place of identification with an occupation.
(Often, of course, but by no means invariably, the school
subject has vocational implications.) The school curriculum
teaches a pupil the kind of person he is. (Often, because of
inappropriate content or misleading methods of examining
his mastery of it, it teaches him falsehood about himself – but
that is another matter.) The price of any curriculum is the
other curriculum that might have been, the other person the
pupil might have known as himself.

And to a still greater extent, subjects provide *teachers* with
a personal anchorage, a sense of who they are and what they
stand for. Their attachment to their subject is nurtured through
subject organizations; and teachers in schools, and particularly
in universities, may even feel that their first loyalty is to their
subject rather than to the organization which employs them.
Scientists and social scientists in industry and the civil service
may become fretful if they are not allowed to publish; their
prime concern is to acquit themselves before their fellow
specialists rather than before their employers. And many
teachers in schools may value recognition in their subject at
least as much as recognition in their schools – and membership
of CSE panels, examination boards, national and local subject
organizations, as well as contributions to various professional
journals, may enable them to gain recognition of this kind.

Curricular changes often involve new social rôles for
teachers, threats to an established source of identity. (Secondary
school reorganization is disturbing for the same reason.) At
best they may be required to become rôle-hybrids, operating
on the margin of their intellectual discipline or in fields conti-
guous to it. For decades educationists have urged, like Professor
Kerr in his paper, shifts to 'broader groupings of knowledge'. The difficulty has been that we have been trying
to change established social, as well as intellectual, systems.

Curriculum innovation requires migrations of subject specialists to unfamiliar activities, to which no recognized, prestigeful labels are attached. Migrants may feel their status threatened, and cling as far as possible to former modes of operation. I suspect that the migration of classics graduates into history and geography, when these were new school subjects, did great harm; history and geography were taught as much like conjugations and declensions as possible, and quite inappropriate modes of 'prep' were required, suitable for a piece of Latin prose, but grotesque in relation to understanding history and geography. We have evidence that this kind of conservatism on the part of subject migrants has led to exciting developments in new subjects – for instance in the growth of psychology in nineteenth century Germany, when physiologists migrated to philosophy and turned it into experimental psychology.[5] But when we develop new subjects, or encourage new combinations of subjects, in our schools, I suspect that a more deliberate preparation of migrants is required. I believe, incidentally, that one of the great obstacles to the development of education as a university study has been the tendency of, say, mathematicians, or linguists who migrate to education to cling to their identity as mathematicians or linguists. Rôle-hybridization in this sphere has not, in my view, been spectacularly successful.

A new subject requires not only suitable recruits, who can tolerate status ambiguities and confusion of identity, it requires an ideology, perhaps a utopia. Many curriculum courses in colleges of education and university departments of education do in fact induct student teachers into subject ideologies and utopias. Unvalidated claims are made for the subjects' potency and effectiveness in attaining particular ends. Well-established subjects usually make do with an unsystematic collection of parables and heroic myths; an emerging subject is more vulnerable and requires a more cogent presentation of its case. The task of curriculum evaluation is really the examination of the claims of subject ideologies. But without their initial extravagant and even fanciful claims, many new sub-

jects and school activities of promise would never become
established.

Sociological investigation, then, may deepen our understanding of the school curriculum as a social system. I have
suggested that academic subjects are bureaucracies; and they
can be studied in the way that we study industrial and mlitary
bureaucracies. We can examine the recruitment to leadership
positions, the distinction between formal and informal leadership, the sources of innovation and of resistance to change, the
modes of communication, the differentiations of status and
their consequences. And, of course, a modern curriculum,
through its sheer complexity, gives rise to more bureaucracy,
calling for co-ordinators, administrators, who organize the
activities of diverse specialists. The consequences of curriculum
change for the bureaucratic development of schools is an
inquiry long overdue.

I began by casting doubt on the contribution that sociology
can make to the determination of curriculum objectives. More
specifically, I was doubtful about the particular way in which
this has been attempted in the past. I should like to return to
this topic, because although it has been done badly, even
dangerously, in the past, sociology in a more modest way may
have some contribution to make in the future.

Professor Kerr suggested that there were three major sources
of data for deciding curriculum objectives: information about
the needs and interests of pupils, 'the social conditions and
problems which the children are likely to encounter', and the
nature of the subject matter and appropriate forms of learning.
Clearly sociologists might be expected to contribute information about the social conditions which children are likely to
encounter. But the children are going to encounter social
conditions over the next fifty or sixty years. The sociologist
must therefore assume a prophetic rôle.

I am sure he is equal to doing so. From his analysis of social
change he must indicate the likely shape of the future, of which
the curriculum must take account. Very summarily I will refer
to five tendencies of modern society that can be extrapolated

to guide our reflections on curriculum reform. They are: the declining demand for unskilled labour, the greater expectation of life, the rapid obsolescence of knowledge, the earlier physical (and perhaps emotional and intellectual) maturing of the young, and the ever lessening distinction between the social rôles of men and women.

Our curricula are still geared to a society in which the majority would be engaged in manual work, knowledge once acquired had a permanent value, the age of puberty was seventeen, life was over at forty, and Father never bathed the baby.

The reduced demand for manual labour and the opportunities for more sophisticated skills and personal qualities mean that we have to discover how more academic curricula can be made to work with less naturally gifted people, at least at some stage in their lives. I think there is little doubt that many children in our secondary modern schools are working well below their true capacities. CSE may help to remedy this. The problem is to teach academic courses not only to those who, for a variety of reasons, already possess the qualities of memory, verbal ability and motivation which teachers have been able with comparative ease to exploit.

The rapid obsolescence of knowledge means that the style and content of the curriculum must change, too – as, indeed, they are doing, particularly at more advanced levels of university work. Above all the child must learn how to learn: he must be inducted into subjects which are essentially a way of inquiry rather than a collection of factual information.

The blurring of the distinction between the sex rôles is a trend which we may or may not approve, but it is likely to continue. In their recent investigations in Nottingham the Newsons found that there had been 'a massive change in the masculine rôle' within the home over the past thirty years.[6] Margaret Mead has reached similar conclusions, with regret, from her observations of the American social scene.[7] These trends suggest not simply that more girls do engineering, but that more boys engage in a new version of domestic science.

We have not yet come to terms in our educational and social arrangements with the longer expectation of life and the earlier maturing of the young. The ages at which we customarily do a great many things – receive our education, marry, settle to a career, retire – are appropriate to social and psychological circumstances which no longer obtain.

We probably need to rephase the life-cycle of man in contemporary society. We are doing too many things at the wrong time – including a good deal of our educational effort. We impose a uniformity on the life-cycle which is no longer either appropriate or necessary. We have gradually assimilated the entire population to the life-cycle of the medieval knight.

While there are reasons for keeping the young at school and off the labour market, there is no immutable reason why redundancy should not be spread, or at least staggered, over the life-span; why retirement ages should not be variable, according to inclination and rates of declining competence; and why men and women in their middle years should not return to educational institutions both for personal renewal and re-equipment for the changing character of their employment.

With ample provision for later educational opportunities I think we could devise more realistic curricula for the various episodes of education. For some a straight run through until their middle twenties would still be appropriate. Many others would return, after a briefer education, in accordance with their changing interests and aspirations. The late thirties would probably be the time for the higher education of most women. It seems to me ludicrous to expect young women who first menstruate at eleven to pay close attention to academic studies until their early twenties, and we need no longer assume that by forty all life will have deserted them. There are probably many men of talent but early physical maturity who might follow a similar pattern, returning to formal education when their families were off their hands.

I suggest, then, that we should think of curricula appropriate to a far more flexible social and educational order; that we should consider the possibilities of a more episodic type of

education; that we should think of curricula which are relevant
to the real (and changing) nature of knowledge, man and
society.

I have left the question of curriculum evaluation to the end,
principally because of its difficulty. (The subject really requires
a paper to itself.) I have already indicated that the sociologist's appreciation of the nature of social facts is likely to
make him sceptical about the extent to which a curriculum
can achieve social objectives. I will now try to carry this point
further.

Many areas of the school curriculum have implicit or
explicit social objectives. History, human geography, and
social studies may aim at promoting social tolerance, domestic
science at improving family relationships, literary studies at
more positive and creative uses of leisure. Evaluation in this
field is long-term, although at a more psychological level (for
example, in assessing attitude change) evaluation may be
attempted after a particular course of studies has been completed. An interesting example of such evaluation was published
in the British Journal of Educational Psychology in 1961,
reporting changes in attitudes to negroes resulting from different
syllabuses in human geography.[8]

It may be that our school curricula are powerful agents of
'bourgeoisification' – that domestic science and perhaps
literary studies inculcate middle-class values and prescribe
middle-class modes of behaviour. I am not concerned with the
morality of such a process. But it would be interesting to
examine the social values implicit (and explicit) in our curricula, and the extent to which they are effectively transmitted
and influence behaviour. Wholesale bourgeoisification may be
a desirable curriculum objective; some sociologists tell us that
rapid bourgeoisification is one of the salient social processes of
our day. The part played by school curricula in this process is
still obscure.

Although there are very considerable problems of technique
in investigating social changes and relating them to school

curricula, the main difficulty is an inadequate sociological and educational theory to guide our investigations. In this field simple and naïve *post hoc propter hoc* interpretations have usually sufficed. Thus the teaching of hygiene in the later nineteenth century has been held to account for the rapid improvement in the nation's health that occurred at that time. Health legislation, sanitary technology, and increasing affluence may in fact have been much more decisive.

Curriculum reform has often been expected to produce far-reaching social change. One of the most interesting examples of this belief that I know occurred in a paper presented to the National Association for the Promotion of Social Science in 1873. Migration was under discussion, and the failure of rural labourers to move into the towns was attributed to defects in the school geography syllabus. The problem was stated thus: 'the shores of the Dead Sea, and the distance in Jewish measurement from Jerusalem to Jericho, is far better known to the children of our working classes than the geography of the Midlands or the road from Exeter to Bristol, or any other of our great centres of industry'.[9] But migration is a social fact, and we are likely to understand it when we examine the related facts of economic organization rather than the teaching of geography in our schools.

Recent investigations of the use of leisure are a warning against using education as a simple predictor of social change. Thus in both England and America research has consistently failed to show that education makes much difference to what viewers choose to watch on television. Only at the very highest levels does education appear to be effective in differentiating consumers of the mass media. (In a study carried out in Detroit with 1,345 subjects, only 19 had significantly 'superior' viewing habits: of these, 16 were university professors!) The more highly educated tend to make different verbal statements about their preferences – they have learned what they ought to like and what they ought to feel about culture, but their actual behaviour is rather differently determined.[10] (We may find the same in studies of tolerance. The correlation with educational level which has often been demonstrated depends on verbal statements.)

Actual leisure-time behaviour appears to be related to other, structural factors – the length of the working week is particularly relevant. Particular forms of education are only marginally relevant, a residual category in explanation.

The work of evaluating curricula from the point of view of social objectives has scarcely begun. When it *is* done, it should be guided by a more sophisticated sociological theory than has been the case in the past. And even if the curriculum turns out to be no more than a residual category in explaining social changes, it is not entirely negligible and merits close examination.

References

1 Fred Clarke, *Freedom in the Educative Society*, University of London Press, 1948.
2 Cf. Jacques Barzun, *The House of Intellect*, Secker and Warburg, 1959, p. 22.
3 E.g. Derek J. de Solla Price, *Little Science Big Science*, Columbia University Press, 1963; W. O. Hagstrom, *The Scientific Community*, Basic Books, 1965.
4 E.g. J. Ben-David, 'Rôles and Innovation in Medicine', *American Journal of Sociology*, vol. 65, 1960.
5 J. Ben-David, 'Social Factors in the Origins of a New Science', *American Sociological Review*, vol. 31, 1966.
6 John and Elizabeth Newson, *Infant Care in an Urban Community*, Allen and Unwin, 1963.
7 Margaret Mead, *Male and Female*, Penguin Books, 1962.
8 H. M. Williams, 'Changes in Attitudes towards West African Negroes', *British Journal of Educational Psychology*, 1961.
9 A. H. Hill, 'Impediments to the Circulation of Labour', Transactions N.A.P. *Social Science*, 1873.
10 For a full discussion of these issues, see D. McQuail, 'Mass Culture, Mass Media, and Minority Taste', paper read to the Conference of the British Sociological Association, April, 1967.

Index